WHAT
YOUNG PEOPLE
NEED
TO KNOW ABOUT MONEY

ROMA DHAMEJA

ACKNOWLEDGEMENTS

Writing a book has been a journey. It has made me think about the years of knowledge I have shared with my wonderful students regarding finances and money. How we have tried to make sense of a rapidly changing world. We've even been able to try out some of the activities in this book. It has inspired me to speak with friends about their hopes and dreams for their children and ways to confidently discuss personal finance with them. Therefore I want to thank all the people who have helped me put this book together, my students, my friends and my family.

My parents came to the UK in the 60s and learnt about finances the hard way, with very little money in their pocket but dreams that kept them going. I have learnt a lot from that. They had little formal schooling and my mother often laughs about how she, who was denied the chance to go to school, is now the mother of a woman who has been an educator for over a decade. What they lacked in formal education, they both more than made up for in entrepreneurial spirit. So, to my parents, thank you for lighting the fire in me that keeps motivating me to do more. And to my nieces, I hope you will carry this fire forward. I love you all.

HOW TO USE THIS BOOK

This book is yours to use as you wish. If you want to start at the start and work your way through it, go right ahead. The chapters do build on each other in that way. If you feel you know some of the content then skip forward. If you want to just dip in and out of it as and when you need, then that is fine too. Check out the contents page and use the information when you need it. The point is, I want it to be useful and for you to decide. I want young people to be informed and I don't want financial literacy to be based on luck depending on where you were born, which school you were at or how confident your family are about talking about money.

If you are a parent, carer or teacher who wants to use these activities with your young people, great! Feel free to add in your own examples and bring the content to life. I hope you have fun. Because understanding how all this works is interesting and can make your life a whole lot easier. Take that from someone who has had to figure it out along the way!

CONTENTS

Personal Finance

6

The Economy

90

The World of Work

136

Conclusion

172

Personal Finance

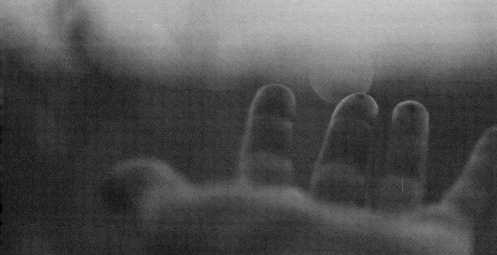

CHAPTER - 01

Wants and Needs

In this chapter, we will look at:

- The difference between a want and a need
- How societies may differ in their wants and needs
- How needs are identified by the government
- Deciding on wants and needs in your life
- Minimalism and its impact on society

Differentiating Between Wants and Needs:

Needs refer to goods and services we must have in order to survive.

Wants are desires for goods and services we would like to have but do not need in order to survive.

Many wants can be seen as needs because we cannot imagine living in modern society without them, for example, the internet. Although you don't need access to the internet to survive, you may struggle to get employment without it and then provide for your basic needs. This may also apply to a mobile phone.

Question What are some things you believe you couldn't live without, even if they are unnecessary for your survival?

List some of your needs and wants below in the table. If you are unsure, you can add some to the unsure column—these may be items such as the internet. You understand you don't need the internet to survive but would struggle to live in modern society without it.

Needs Goods or services needed for survival	Unsure	Wants Nice to have but not needed to live

Some ideas are highlighted in the table below

Needs Goods or services needed for survival	Unsure	Wants Nice to have but not needed to live
Accommodation	Internet	Takeaway once a week
Clothing	Mobile phone	Trips to the cinema
		Holiday once a year

What Societies Around the World Define as Wants and Needs

What societies consider to be wants and needs can vary significantly. In developed countries such as the UK, we might consider a minimum of seven sets of clothes or a full wardrobe a need; however, in countries where people suffer from poverty, one set of clothes may be enough.

Activity - 2

Look at your needs column in the table above. What are your expectations with these needs? For instance, under accommodation, is a 3-bedroom house what you consider to be the basic standard of living for it to fulfil your need? Or do you feel you need a 5-bedroom house?

Visit Gapminder www.gapminder.org/dollar-street. This tool allows you to compare different factors, such as cars and bathrooms across the world. Select the items you want to compare and the countries you want to compare for images to appear. This should give you an indication of standards of living around the world and what they may consider as a need and a want.

How Needs Are Identified By the Government

The Consumer Price Index is a group of goods that the government considers to be commonly needed by individuals in the UK. The government uses it to measure the average change in prices over time of the basket of goods and services they feel households in the UK need. This helps the government measure inflation, which refers to how prices are changing over time (something we will look at later in the book).

The basket of goods is reviewed each year to determine necessary items. Items are often removed and replaced by others that reflect what people buy. For instance, as the UK becomes more conscious of the environmental impact our way of life causes, reusable mugs and water bottles have been added to the basket of goods.

Look at the categories included in the basket of goods that are listed below:

- ➲ **Are there any categories you would not expect to be there?**
- ➲ **Are they all considered needs?**

Food & non-alcoholic beverages	Transport
Alcohol & tobacco	Communication
Clothing & footwear	Recreation & culture
Housing & household services	Education
Furniture & household goods	Restaurants & Hotels
Health	

Think of a couple of items you would expect in each category and jot them down.

EXTENSION ACTIVITY

If you would like to have a look at the list of basket of goods, this can be found by typing the following into Google: 'Consumer price inflation basket of goods and services.' [1]

Do any of the items in the list surprise you?

---

1   Office for National Statistics, Consumer price inflation basket of goods and services,
     https://www.ons.gov.uk/economy/inflationandpriceindices/datasets/consumerpriceinflationbasketofgoodsandservices

Review the items below. The items in the first column were added to the basket of goods in 2021. The items in the second column were taken out of the basket of goods. Do you agree with these decisions? Why? Why not?

Items added to the basket of goods in 2021	Items removed from the basket of goods in 2021
Couscous	Restaurant sandwiches - removed to reflect that more people were having lunch at home because of COVID-19 and not going into the office
Men's and Women's loungewear (why do you think this would have been added in 2021 during the COVID-19 pandemic?)	White chocolate bars - replaced by more popular chocolate such as Maltesers
Smartwatch	Fruit smoothies - replaced by fruit and vegetable smoothies combined
Coffee Sachets	Ground coffee

Deciding on Wants and Needs in Your Own Life

The discussions and activities above should have you thinking about needs and wants at a deeper level and questioning purchasing decisions. The next activity requires you to apply this to how you imagine your life.

Complete a mind map using the categories in Activity 3 that outlines what you want your life to look like in the future. I would suggest not going too far in the future but if you are 18 for instance you might want to pick an age in your mid 20s. What needs and wants would you have in your life? Would you like to have moved out? Be sharing a flat with a friend? Have your own car? How often would you like to go shopping for clothes? At this point, the mind map can be very vague but should get you thinking about the needs and wants you imagine in your own life as you get older. This mind map will help you calculate your cost of living in the "Cost of Living" chapter later in the book.

Minimalism

Minimalism is a philosophy that encourages people to live with less and have a few quality items that they enjoy. This should then lead to lower debt for people and a simpler, calmer life. For many it is a step towards financial freedom – where an individual has enough money to pay for their expenses for the rest of their life.

Go to YouTube and watch the video "What is Minimalism" by Joshua Becker, which is 2 minutes 38 seconds long. Don't worry if you can't find it. You will still find a range of videos explaining what minimalism is.

QUESTIONS

Why do you think minimalism is becoming more and more popular amongst people?

In May 2021, The Money Charity, found that the average household credit card debt was £1,938. How might this affect the rise of minimalism?

Why might minimalism be difficult to follow?

Would you want to be a minimalist?

Go back to your mind map from activity 6, do you want to make any changes?

In Summary

This chapter has identified wants and needs and given you opportunities to identify your own. The chapter has also highlighted the variation in wants and needs depending on where people live. We have explored how the government uses the Consumer Price Index and identifies the wants and needs of an average family in the UK to monitor inflation. Finally, we have looked at the rise of minimalism, which tries to minimise the desire for wants.

CHAPTER - 02

Cost of Living

In this chapter, we will look at:

- How to calculate the cost of living for the life you want to live
- The costs for different goods and services
- How cost-of-living changes during a lifetime

Cost of living is defined as: The amount of money needed to cover expenses (or costs) for living a certain way.

Many young people leave school without a realistic understanding of how much things cost, simply because they have not started purchasing certain goods or services yet. You may know things like the price of groceries, but other expenses such as insurance, internet, and council tax may not be so clear. Without taking the time to consider the cost of living, young people may have unrealistic expectations of the life they can afford in the future and thus lack a sense of satisfaction if those expectations aren't met.

The following exercise aims to build:

Awareness:

The activities below will allow you time to get clear about the choices you will need to make later in your life about how you want to live and build awareness of these choices.

Motivation:

Once you are clear about the life you want to live and how much it will cost you, this gives you a clear goal to work towards.

Expectations:

Use this activity to question expectations. For instance, if you anticipate spending £500 on clothes each month and owning the latest technology, you may question whether those purchases are practical or necessary. You could also think about what saving this money would allow you to do instead (e.g., invest in travelling, buying your first property, etc.)

Decision-making:

Overall, the activity should help you make better and more informed decisions as you shape your adult life. Once you understand your wants and needs (covered at the start of this book), you should be making conscious purchases that are in line with your goal.

Changes in the Cost of Living During a Lifetime

Cost of living often changes with age (see diagram below). When people are very young, their parents/carers cover their costs. As they get older, they may start taking responsibility for their costs by earning money for doing chores or getting a part-time job and then spending that money on things they enjoy. As they move through their 20s they may cover their own cost of living almost entirely. This rise in the cost of living will continue if and when they decide to have a family. Once their children leave home, their cost of living is likely to fall again as they spend less on everyday items such as food. Many people also downsize their homes at this point to reduce bills as their children move out.

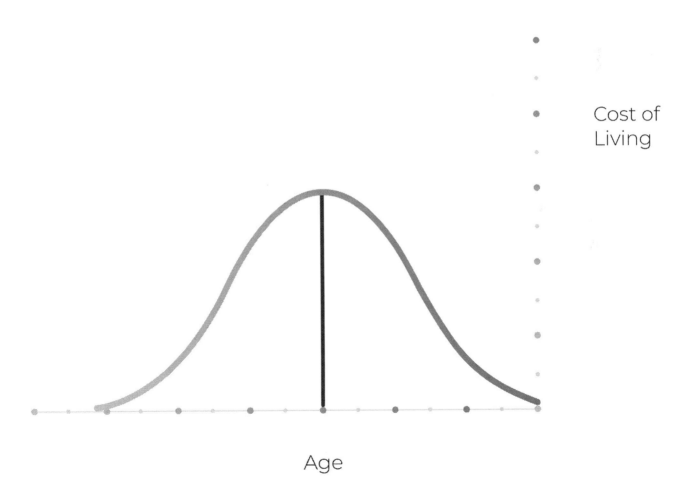

Cost of Living

Age

Pick an age for which you would like to calculate a cost of living. It is best not to go too far into the future as costs for items are likely to change. The author would recommend an age in your 20s, at which point most imagine living independently with a housemate, perhaps. Complete a mind map using the below categories to imagine your future life. (If you completed this in the "Wants and Needs" chapter, you should make sure you have it on hand and consider the following Qs).

Some questions to think about whilst completing your mind map:

Do you want to live in a city or rural area? As costs are likely to vary.

The average age of buying a house in the UK is 32-34. Therefore, it is likely that you will rent accommodation in your 20s. Do you want to share a house or live by yourself? Living by yourself is likely to be more expensive as you cannot split the bills with your housemate.

Do you wish to have a car? Is this necessary? For instance, many cities are pedestrianised, or it is very difficult to drive into them, such as Oxford, London, or Nottingham. Therefore, would public transport be better? More cost-effective?

Can you cook, and if not, this should be a skill you learn, as eating out each day is likely to be costly. No one is expecting you to be a professional chef, but knowing how to cook five simple dishes could save you a lot of money and be a healthier way of eating.

Many young people forget to factor in things they enjoy, for instance exercise and memberships. Do you want to join a gym? Partake in a sport regularly? Do you love going to the movies? These activities cost money and should be factored in.

Calculating Cost of Living

Complete the cost-of-living exercise that follows. We recommend that you take the time to look through the table and instructions a couple of times before you start.

Calculate the costs on a monthly basis below in the table for the life you have imagined for yourself in Activity 1. Some guidance has been provided in the notes under the table

NOTE

You have been asked to calculate a third of your salary to go towards taxes. This may seem excessive; however, costs for emergencies and savings have not been included, so makes room for those.

Cost of Living Exercise

Please note all costs in the table below are monthly.

Rent or Mortgage	Utilities Bills	Groceries	Eating & drinking out	Clothes	Travel	Memberships	Phone Bill	Other	Total Monthly Outgoing

Notes to Complete the Table

Rent/Mortgage: Use a site like Zoopla.co.uk to help you search for somewhere you would like to.

If you want a calculation for a mortgage, you could use this tool on the Money Advice Service website tools/mortgage-calculator.

Utilities: The following advice from Money Saving Expert might come in handy

https://www.moneyhelper.org.uk/en/homes/buying-a-home/mortgage-calculator?source=mas#

Groceries: You could visit Asda, Tesco, Aldi, or any of the other supermarket websites to calculate costs.

Eating and Drinking Out: You can go onto some of your favourite restaurant websites and see how much a meal and drinks cost. Or you can use the averages calculated in this research on Nimble Fins, which were updated in March 2021 at:

https://www.nimblefins.co.uk/average-uk-household-cost-food

Clothes: A simple glance at a few online stores will give you some ideas.

Travel: Look at the cost of bus or rail travel. Many people avoid getting a car straight away to avoid costs of petrol, car insurance, and actually purchasing and maintaining the car. Nerd Wallet gives you the average cost of running a car which you can use as a basis and is available at:

https://www.nerdwallet.com/uk/personal-finance/cost-of-car-ownership/#what-our-survey-reveals-the-average-running-cost-of-a-car-in-the-uk.

Note this includes average fuel costs and monthly car payments sometimes.

Membership/Subscriptions: This might be for the gym, magazine subscriptions, Netflix, or Sky, etc.

Phone Bill: Monthly phone bills will vary depending on what plan you sign up for, but a website like Money Supermarket can give you an idea

Holidays: Airbnb and Expedia and TUI's Holiday spending money calculator should give you a good idea.

Average salary in the UK

https://www.findcourses.co.uk/jobs/

You can use the above website to look at how much your chosen career will pay on average. It also shows if there is a gender gap in the profession.

Step 01   **Complete the table with monthly costs**

Step 02   **Calculate Yearly outgoings by multiplying the monthly ones by 12**

Total Monthly Outgoings x 12 =

Step 03   **Add other possible yearly costs to this figure**

Holidays: Airbnb and Expedia and TUI's Holiday spending money calculator should give you a good idea.

Big purchases: Such as TV, washing machine, fridge, and any electricals. Although you won't buy a tv, every year it is likely you will need one electrical item, so it is best to put some money aside for one.

Once you know how much these yearly costs are add them to the figure in Step 2

Step 04   **Figure out how much you need to earn**

Take the final sum from Step 3 and add a third (taxes etc.) For instance, if my total yearly outgoings come to £15000, I would calculate the following 15,000/2 x 3 = which means I need to earn £22,500 per annum.

EXTENSION ACTIVITY

Once you have completed the cost of living exercise, search online for the average salary of someone in the profession you would like to join. Does the salary cover your predicted cost of living? Don't forget your salary is taxed, so you need to take away a third of the stated salary as what remains will be in your bank account to cover your costs (take home salary).

Some stats to help you:

According to Revolut, in 2020 the average cost of living in the UK is as follows:

- **£2,249** per month for a single person
- **£3,803** per month for a family of four

CHAPTER - 03

Interest Rates

In this chapter, we will cover:

- What interest rates are
- How high and low interest rates determine how we spend and save
- Identify the different ways interest rates affect our decisions
- What is compound interest and how does it differ from normal interest

An **Interest Rate** is the cost of borrowing money and the reward for saving. When individuals borrow money for purchases such as a TV or a house, interest rates determine how much they pay back to the bank, as interest is the charge for borrowing. So if interest rates are 5% and you borrow £100, you will end up paying back £105 after one year. Similarly, you earn interest for saving, so if you save £100 and interest rates are 5%, then you will make £5 on your saving, giving you £105 in the bank over time.

Interest rates play a vital part in the financial health of adults. When used effectively, they can help individuals save money for a later date and avoid unnecessary costs.

The **Bank of England** sets the base rate for interest rates in the UK, which influences the rate set by financial institutions, such as high street banks. If the base rate rises, the chances are the banks will increase their interest rates. The Bank of England uses interest rates to control spending. For example, when the country is coming out of a recession, it will set the base rate as very low (post-COVID-19 interest rate was 0.1%) so that people borrow more money and buy things. In turn, this stimulates the economy, and eventually leads to more employment and wealth, in theory. If the population has already borrowed a lot of money, the Bank of England may try to control spending by increasing interest rates, so people stop borrowing money to purchase goods, slowing the economy down. It's important to note that banks' individual levels of interest will vary from bank to bank and even for each account that they offer.

Questions

Why do you think interest rates will become important to you in the future?

What types of decisions do you think are determined by them? For example, what purchasing and saving decisions would interest rates become a central factor for?

Think about if you are saving for a house, do you want interest rates to be high or low?

Below are some decisions that interest rates impact.

Please note this is not a complete list but gives some examples.

Decisions affected by interest rates:

- The bank you decide to use
- The credit card you get in the future
- The savings account you use and where you decide to save money
- If you decide to save or spend at a particular time
- Whether you buy products outright or pay for them in instalments
- When you buy a house

Paying in instalments for items

Unless you have saved up to buy a product outright, you may need to borrow money to purchase major items, such as large electrical items. Many stores offer the ability to pay in instalments over a period. These options often come with interest payments, and you should look out for these and try to aim for the lowest level of interest on these items as possible.

Credit cards

Once a person turns 18, they are likely to be offered a credit card. Credit cards offer people the ability to use money they don't yet have and pay it back later. Many banks and credit card companies offer a credit card with no interest to begin with, later adding interest when the customer can no longer be bothered to change their credit card provider. This is something to look out for.

When saving and wanting to earn interest

Just like credit cards, savings accounts can vary in interest too. Everyday accounts used to withdraw cash to do your daily shopping are unlikely to offer high rewards for saving. Many banks will offer better interest rates if you make regular payments into your savings account and agree not to withdraw money from it for a set period.

What is compound interest?

Compound interest is known as interest on interest. The previous examples suggest that in a current account that you use daily, you may get £105 at the end of the year if you were making 5% interest because the interest is calculated on the principal amount (the money you initially put down - £100.) Compound interest, on the other hand, gains interest on the interest earnt, as well as on the principal amount. Therefore, in the second year, your interest will be calculated on the principal of £105. And so on each year. Compound interest accounts can compound daily, monthly, or annually, and as a result, compound interest grows a lot faster than simple interest.

It is important to note that compound interest can hurt you when you borrow money on loans such as mortgages. Therefore, it is imperative to pay these off as soon as practically possible.

Interest Rates Can Be Fixed or Variable!

Fixed interest rates stay the same for the set period of time of the loan or its entirety.

Variable interest rates can change over time.

When interest rates are low, people tend to borrow at a fixed interest rate since it is likely to rise in the future. Similarly, if interest rates are high, people may go for a variable rate on their loan, hoping the interest rate will fall. Of course you can never be certain what will happen to interest in the future so your decision carries a level of risk.

In Summary

Interest affects everyone, whether you are spending money or saving it. Compound interest rewards savings and investment in a significant way than normal interest and should be considered when making decisions about saving.

CHAPTER - 04

Saving and Savings Accounts

In this chapter, we will cover:

⧽ The options you have once you have money

⧽ Why you should save

⧽ Different savings accounts and what they can offer

⧽ The relationships between savings, inflation, and interest rates.

A person has many possibilities when they have money, which include:

- Spending on goods
- Spending on services
- Spending on travel and experiences
- Donating
- Lending
- Saving

QUESTION

Brainstorm all the reasons you may want to save money below:

Some reasons to save may include:

- For purchase of high-value items such as a car
- For investment in a business/stocks and shares
- To start a business
- To put a deposit down on a house
- To save for emergencies
- To save for a holiday
- To make a donation

Savings and Depreciation

Depreciation is a reduction in the value of an item or currency over time. For items, this is particularly due to wear and tear.

When saving money, if a person does not need immediate access to their funds, it is best to look for a savings account rather than keeping the money in a current account used for everyday purchases. This is because savings accounts (depending on the one you pick) can give you a higher interest on savings. Remember, interest is the reward for saving.

If you have reviewed the inflation chapter in this book, you know that goods and services get more expensive over time. This means that if you are saving money unless it also increases in line with interest, you will be able to buy less with it in the future (as prices for things you want to buy will rise). This is depreciation, where money is worth less in the future than it is now. An example of this is if you went grocery shopping with £10 today and then 10 years later spend the same amount again, you'll be able to buy a lot less because items will have gotten more expensive.

The Bank of England aims for 2% inflation, so if you put your savings into a current bank account with 0.5% interest, it will be worth less over time because goods are now more expensive than the money you have in your account!

In order to avoid this, you will want to try to find a savings account that can at least keep up with inflation.

Getting Into the Habit of Saving

It is good to get into the habit of saving early on. Even if you have a part-time job while at school, it is wise to set yourself small savings goals. These can be something like 5% of your income and grow as your income increases. These habits will then solidify, and it will be easier for you to save for larger items, such as a car or a house as you get older.

You can set yourself short-term and long-term goals for saving. A short-term saving goal might be for savings that are accessed regularly for birthday treats, nights out, etc.

Longer-term savings are for things like a wedding, holidays, or a house.

Also, think about an emergency savings fund in case of a broken bike or car. You may want to save a pot of money for these things, so you don't have to worry about not having enough money for unexpected costs/emergencies.

Savings Accounts

Why are savings accounts beneficial?

1. They can help you earn more interest on your savings than inflation and more than a regular account.
2. They help you get into the habit of putting money aside in savings.
3. They can relieve the temptation to spend if your money goes directly into a savings account, which you cannot withdraw from for a period of time, therefore curbing impulse buying. If withdrawn early you can face penalties or lose your interest gains.

Drawbacks to savings accounts

Many require customers to put a minimum amount in monthly. This can be as little as £1 a month to £1000s a month.

Many also require that you do not withdraw money for a set amount of time from 1 to 10 years or more!

Individual Savings Account (ISA)

This is a tax-free account in which you can save a certain amount each financial year without paying tax. In 2020/2021, for instance, this amount is £20,000. A financial year is from 6th April to 5th April the following year.

There are 3 types of ISA Accounts:

1. An instant access ISA - This allows people to access money whenever they like (so if the person saving needs to withdraw money within the year they can).

2. A fixed-term ISA - Means a person puts in money and doesn't withdraw it for a set period of time.

3. Stocks and Shares ISA - Stocks and shares accounts which basically use the money invested in stocks and shares as part of a person's non-taxed ISA savings. (We will look at investing in stocks and shares later in the book.)

Choosing a Savings Account

Before choosing and opening a savings account, a person must be clear about how much they want to save each month, where this money will come from, and how long they plan to save without withdrawing. Savings accounts can vary on a variety of factors, such as:

- **Interest rate** – How much the bank gives you for saving with them
- **Withdrawals** – How often you can take out money
- **Minimum monthly payment** – How much you have to put into savings each month

Look at the savings accounts below and list the advantages and disadvantages of each by completing the table.

QUESTION

Would a person at the age of 20, 25, and 45 go for different options? This is likely, as a person often gains a steadier stream of income as they get older and can feel more confident in how much they can put into savings regularly.

	Savings Account 1	Savings Account 2	Saving Accounts 3
Interest	2.5%	3.5%	7%
Minimum monthly payment	£1	£50	£1000
No withdrawals	For up to 1 year	3 years	5 years
Advantages			
Disadvantages			
Ideal for?			
Young people (18-25), slightly older or those more established in their careers in the 30s/40s/50s perhaps?			

A completed table has been provided for you below to check answers.

	Savings Account 1	Savings Account 2	Saving Accounts 3
Interest	2.5%	3.5%	7%
Minimum monthly payment	£1	£50	£1000
No withdrawals	For up to 1 year	3 years	5 years
Advantages	Low monthly payments so unlikely to fail to meet these.	Reasonable monthly payments. Above inflation average, so money is holding value.	Large sums are being saved and earning a good amount of interest.
Disadvantages	Interest rate is similar to the government inflation rate target.	A young person may need access to the money sooner if they haven't been working long.	Difficult to access money in case of emergency or will lose interest.
Ideal for?	Student/young person who does not have a lot of money or a steady income, so is uncertain that they can pay in a regular amount. However, having a savings account will get them into good habits to put money aside.	An individual who is starting out in their career, so has an income but not much left at the end of the month once they have paid their bills. Could be saving for a big holiday.	An individual with a steady income saving for a deposit on a house or for their retirement. Can afford to buy immediate needs and wants with current salary and still save.

In Summary

This chapter explains the relationship between savings, interest, and inflation. Your savings need to be protected against inflation to ensure they do not depreciate. Savings accounts offer you a range of options, and when applying for one, it is best to pick one that suits your needs.

CHAPTER - 05

Building a Credit Score

In this chapter, we will look at:

- What a credit score is
- What opportunities a strong credit score allows
- How to develop a strong credit score
- How to check your credit score

A credit score has a large impact on a person's financial security and health. From basics such as allowing a young person to hire a car or rent a room in a shared house or buying a house. A person's credit score allows a person to take advantage of many opportunities.

What is credit?

Credit is the ability to borrow money or access goods or services with the understanding that you'll pay later. Step Change, the debt charity, reported that over 7 million people in Britain turn to credit to pay for their everyday essentials at least occasionally and over 13 million would need to borrow money to cover emergency costs.[2] Therefore, the ability to gain credit is important.

What is a credit score?

A credit score is a number that depicts a consumer's creditworthiness (how good they are to lend money to). It's like a CV for your finances. It tells lenders how well you have managed your money in the past. Some credit checking companies give a score between 0-999 and others between 300-850. Whichever scale they choose, the higher the number, the better the score, and the more likely the person is to be lent money from a financial institution.

Some factors a credit score is based on:

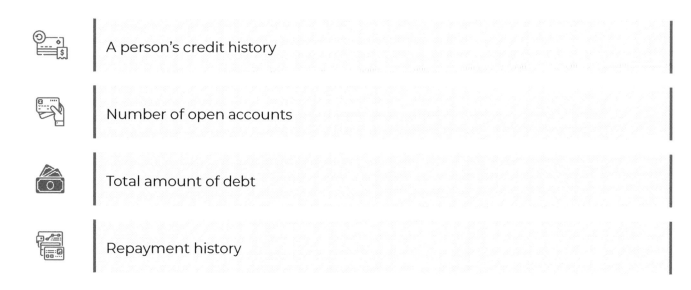

A person's credit history

Number of open accounts

Total amount of debt

Repayment history

---

2   Step Change, The credit safety net: consumer trends and problem debt,
      https://www.stepchange.org/policy-and-research/consumer-credit-trends-and-debt.aspx

Is the best thing not to have a credit card and ensure I never borrow money?

It's important to know that this is not the case. A bank needs to see how creditworthy an individual is so evidence of paying off their debts is necessary. Therefore, no credit card means a weak credit score.

The best way to use a credit card is to use it for small amounts to start with, which you can pay off in time for your monthly payments.

Think about how a bank may check if a person should be given money to borrow? What sort of things would they look at? List your ideas below:

1.
2.
3.
4.

How to develop a good credit score:

You can develop a good credit score by ensuring you do the below:

- ➲ Pay your credit card on time
- ➲ Pay off any debts as soon as possible
- ➲ Minimise how much you borrow
- ➲ Don't open too many accounts

- Don't spend up to your credit limit too often
- Check your credit reports to make sure your information is not compromised
- Develop a credit history over time
- Show a regular source of income
- Never miss a scheduled payment
- Be on the electoral roll
- Have all credit/bills registered to the same address

The above list is also what the bank will check before deciding whether they lend you money. A credit check will consider banking history, average income and spending, and whether you have any other outstanding debts to be paid back.

Large purchases you need a credit score for:

- Phone contract
- Renting property
- Buying a car
- Getting a mortgage to buy a house - A person can get a better mortgage (with lower interest) if they have a better credit score as they are seen as less of a risk.
- A better deal on a credit card - The person is less of a risk (because their credit score shows they are good at paying their debts).
- Better insurance deals on cars, house insurance, etc.
- Easier access to utilities - When young people move out of their parent's house, they need to sign up for utilities such as water, gas, and internet. These companies run credit checks and can demand a deposit that they hold if an individual has a poor credit rating. This is so they can hold some money in case an individual doesn't pay their bills.

Guarantors

The first time a young person buys something on credit (such as getting a flat on rent) they may need a parent or someone older to be a guarantor. Essentially, they are supporting the young person in their request for credit and saying that they will pay the rent/bill if the young person fails to do so. The guarantor too needs a good credit score and of course should be asked before they are named.

In Summary

We have discussed the importance of a credit score and how someone can develop a good credit score. We have also looked at the purchases a good credit score allows you to make. In the next chapter, we will review choosing from different credit cards and the types of cards on offer.

CHAPTER - 06

Debit and Credit Cards

In this chapter, we will cover:

- The difference between debit and credit cards
- When each type of card is normally used
- Understand different credit and debit accounts

Some stats

According to The Money Charity, in February 2021,[3] credit card debt averaged £1962 per household or £1032 per adult. They also noted that a credit card on the average interest would take 24 years and 5 months to repay if making only the minimum repayments each month.

In a world where Klarna (an online payment system that allows shoppers to pay for high street items over 30 days or in 3 instalments) exists, young people are more readily getting credit from their favourite stores. You must be aware of credit, debit, and the impact of shopping habits on your credit scores for the future.

Debit card	Credit
Uses money that you already have. So when you use the debit card to buy something, it withdraws money directly from your account to cover the cost.	When you use a credit card, the amount will be charged to your line of credit, meaning you will pay the bill at a later date, which also gives you more time to pay. You borrow the money from the company you have the credit card with.

Wait, so I can buy things without having the money?

It is important to highlight a few factors here:

- ⮑ You can't get a credit card until you're 18 with a minimum income (varies from provider to provider).

- ⮑ You will be limited as to how much you can borrow (the amount is likely to start off with a couple of hundred pounds and grow over time with your credit score).

- ⮑ You have to pay the money back with interest (interest is covered earlier in this section of the book, and if you have not reviewed it yet, you may need to cover some of the material there.)

- ⮑ Unless paid off, as stated in the contract, it can end up costing a lot of money and get you into debt, meaning you may struggle to get future credit.

- ⮑ But yes! In theory, you can buy something if you don't have the money but are expecting to get it.

---

3   The Money Charity, https://themoneycharity.org.uk/money-statistics/

QUESTION

Why is it better to purchase with the money you have rather than borrowing it on a credit card? List some reasons below:

1.
2.
3.
4.

When to Use Debit and Credit

There is no hard or fast rule here, and it depends very much on a person's personal circumstances. However, a general rule of thumb for debit and credit card use is:

- **Debit Cards** for most purchases, such as grocery shopping, lunch and dinner, and everyday items.
- **Credit Cards** for larger purchases, such as furniture, flights, etc.

Many credit card companies also provide insurance on some purchases, such as flights, so it is worth knowing this so you can make those purchases with your credit card.

Complete the Debit or Credit table below. Would you want to use a debit or credit card to make the below purchases, and why?

Purchase	Debit or credit	Why
A holiday		
Grocery shopping		
A house		
A new pair of shoes		
Cash withdrawal from cash machine on a night out		
Coffee		
To pay for items when abroad		

A completed table can be found here. Please note: the answers are general guides. Some people may use a credit card to pay for their grocery shopping and that is OK! The key thing is to know that you can pay it off within the time specified by the lender.

Purchase	Debit or credit	Why
A holiday	Credit	Items over £100 are usually insured, which can mean the credit card company can cover any cancelled flights and get replacement flights booked
Grocery shopping	Debit	Better to pay for everyday items on a debit card with money you have
A house	Neither!	This would require a mortgage in most cases, which has to be approved by the bank on a case-by-case basis (we will look at this later in the book)
A new pair of shoes	Debit	Better to pay for everyday items on a debit card with money you have
Cash withdrawal from cash machine on a night out	Debit	Most credit cards will charge you for cash withdrawals
Coffee	Debit	Better to pay for everyday items on a debit card with money you have
To pay for items when abroad	Credit	When travelling, credit cards can be a much safer way than carrying cash and also protect you against fraud. (See "Travelling Abroad" chapter)

Can anyone get a credit card?

It is important to highlight the value of a good credit score here. We discuss this in more detail in the section named "Building a credit score." A good credit score allows you to have access to a line of credit. Normally, those who are 18 or over with an income can apply for a credit card. However, the amount they may borrow will depend on their credit score, income, and other factors, which the credit card issuer will decide.

What to look out for in a credit card

Credit cards offer their customers a range of benefits, and the market for credit cards has become competitive. Below are some of the key factors that young people should look out for when looking for a credit card.

Factor	Explanation
APR	Annual Percentage Rate - The cost of borrowing on the card will be a percentage and usually varies between 18-24%
Interest-free period	Most credit cards will offer you an interest-free period to gain customers; however, you should check whether this comes at a price (for example, a higher APR later)
Minimum repayment	Usually, this will be a percentage of the amount borrowed, for example, 3% or an actual sum such as £100, or the company can say whichever is higher out of the two
Annual fee	Some credit card companies charge you a yearly fee for using them
Additional charges	Fees vary for transfer charges for switching credit cards, cash withdrawal charges, and charges to use your credit card abroad.
Loyalty points and rewards	Some credit cards offer you frequent flyer points or other loyalty points that can be exchanged for goods/services
Cash back	Credit card companies may offer you this if you pay your balance off in full and give you some money back.

Compare the credit cards listed in the table below and their advantages and disadvantages, then decide whom it may be suitable for. Consider whether an 18-year-old university student would be best suited to Credit card A, B, or C, or someone older? Would the card be good for someone who travels a lot? Has a high income or lower income?

	Credit Card A	Credit Card B	Credit Card C
No interest period	0 months	6 months	12 months
APR	24%	19.5%	25%
Bonuses	High street retailer vouchers depending on spend	None	Frequent flyer points giving you money off flights in future
Cash withdrawal charge	3%	5%	2%
Minimum repayment	10%	12%	7%
Additional Charges	£50 bank transfer 4% overseas spend	£70 bank transfer 7% for overseas spend	£50 bank transfer 0% for overseas spend
Pros			
Cons			
Who this card may be good/not so good for			
No interest period			

A completed version with some notes has been included below for you to compare your answers.

	Credit Card A	Credit Card B	Credit Card C
No interest period	0 months	6 months	12 months
APR	24%	19.5%	25%
Bonuses	High street retailer vouchers depending on spend	None	Frequent flyer points giving you money off flights in future
Cash withdrawal charge	3%	5%	2%
Minimum repayment	10%	12%	7%
Additional Charges	£50 bank transfer 4% overseas spend	£70 bank transfer 7% for overseas spend	£50 bank transfer 0% for overseas spend
Pros	Good if you feel you need to withdraw cash	Lowest APR out of 3	Good if you feel you need to withdraw cash. Low minimum repayment
Cons	Quite high APR	Short 0% interest and then expensive to move credit card.	High APR, so needs to have someone who can clear balance monthly
Who this card may be good/not so good for	Good for those who regularly use a credit card at high street retailers	High charge of withdrawing cash so not good for those who may need access to cash. Good for those staying local and who rarely use a credit card	Good for people travelling abroad often. High interest means need to be good at managing money and repayments

How do you pay off a credit card?

The easiest way to pay off a credit card is to transfer money from an account that has money in it into your credit card account. For instance, the account that someone receives income into at the start of the month can have an automated payment set up to their credit card. This can be done online or in-person by going into the bank.

Another method might be to pay with cash. For example, if a person has recently had a birthday, some of their relatives might have been kind enough to give them money. They can take this to the bank and pay off their credit card.

The important thing is timing

Most credit card companies have a minimum payment they want the user to pay off each month. It is important to pay this each month on time. Each time a person misses this minimum payment, their credit score decreases since they have failed to meet a payment.

Are store cards the same as credit cards?

In many ways, store cards are very similar to credit cards. Some store cards, however, are for a specific store, which allows you to borrow money to purchase items from that one shop or group of stores only. Most credit cards can be used anywhere.

In Summary

This chapter has specified the difference between credit and debit cards and when a person would use each type of card. It has also shown that credit cards come with a range of options, and when applying for one, a person should consider their current circumstances and what they need from their credit card to identify the right one for them. It also highlights the difference between credit cards and store cards and how some cards may only be available to people who meet certain criteria.

CHAPTER - 07

Loans

In this chapter, we will look at:

- Different loans available
- What to identify when taking out a loan
- Payday loans

At certain points in people's lives, it is common for them to take out a loan. The average house in the UK costs £236,000 according to the Office of National Statistics. Most people don't have that type of money lying around and therefore choose to get a loan to pay for the house and then slowly pay the loan off, in the hope to eventually own the house.

Different loans available

There are different loans that are available to people. These are listed below with a brief description of each one. It is important to note that what is provided and the charges applied to loans vary from provider to provider, so make sure you review the details before getting a loan.

Unsecured loans

This means that you do not have to offer collateral to gain it (for instance, you do not offer your house up to the bank if you miss a payment.)

Personal Loans

Personal loans are provided by most high street banks. Typically, these can be worth anything from a few hundred pounds to several thousands of pounds and usually need to be paid back within 1-5 years. You will need to show a regular income and proof of ID and complete an application for approval. The rate of interest will be determined by various factors such as size of the loan, level of risk, and how long you need it for; however, moneyfacts.co.uk found that the average interest charged on loans of £5000 for 3 years was 7.4% in June 2020.[4]

Borrowing from friends and family

If you can borrow from friends and family, this may help you avoid interest and the threat of negativley affecting your credit score (see chapter on "Building a Credit Score") if you have to miss a payment. Your friends and family also may not charge you interest, which means you pay back exactly what you borrow. However, this is not always a possibility and it is likely to be for small sums of money.

---

4   Money Facts, Loan rates rise as pandemic hits struggling households the hardest,
     https://moneyfacts.co.uk/news/loans/loan-rates-rise-as-pandemic-hits-struggling-households-the-hardest/

Credit Loans

Credit card loans vary in the amount that is offered and also the rate of interest. Essentially, they allow you to buy things using a card with the money you borrow from the bank. Credit cards will have limits set on how much you can borrow depending on your credit history and rating. For a detailed breakdown of this type of loan, please see the chapter on "Credit and debit cards."

Business Loans

Business loans are for commercial entities rather than individuals and can vary in size from a couple of hundred pounds to millions of pounds. They can be both secured (using your business assets as collateral, meaning the bank can take away property or machinery the business owns if not repaid) or unsecured.

Secured Loans

Homeowner Loans

These are available to those who own or partially own a home where the house is put down as security should they not be able to make the loan repayments. This type of loan is usually used to fund home improvements such as a new kitchen, garage etc. Homeowner loans are available for any time period between 1-35 years and people typically borrow up to a certain percent of the value of the property that they are using as security. There is also a detailed process and credit checking that takes place before it is offered. The amount you can borrow depends on income, credit score, age, and several other factors.

Bridging Loans

These types of loans are often used to purchase something whilst you are waiting for money/a payment to come in for something else. For instance, someone moving and wanting to buy a home may get a bridging loan to allow them to do this while waiting for the money to come in from the sale of their previous home. These are usually only offered if a high-value asset (such as a home) is put down as security, and people will usually borrow hundreds of thousands of pounds.

Vehicle Finance

This is a loan specifically for buying a vehicle and the security is the vehicle you buy (so the vehicle will be taken away if you do not meet payments.) Used for cars, motorbikes, vans, caravans, and motorhomes, for example, and these are widely available, but people need to pass a credit check in order to get them.

Debt Consolidation Loans

This is when a person combines multiple loans (e.g., vehicle, credit card, etc.) and takes out one single loan to pay them off and only has one loan to pay back. This will often be because it has lower interest and is simpler to manage. For example, you may have two credit cards that you owe £5000 each to and the interest may be 22%. You could get a loan for £10,000 and 14% interest and pay them off, paying back less interest. If you are hoping to benefit from this it is important you know the details of each loan you are planning to merge and also have a good credit history.

Payday Loans

Payday loans are easily accessible for small amounts of money, but this can also make them dangerous. As they are not difficult to get and have very high-interest rates, it is easy for people to end up in large amounts of debt using payday loans. Because of the large interest rates, it is incredibly important to ensure you pay these back as soon as possible. Some payday loan providers have been criticised for charging interest that is over 1000% when a loan from a high street bank may only have an interest of 25%, for example. They also need to be paid back in a very short window (sometimes two weeks), so the provider can increase interest rates if this does not happen. It is crucial to avoid these types of loan providers as they are often seen as predatory and can really damage your credit rating.

Summary

There are many forms of loan an individual can take out during their lifetime. The key factors to be considered are their credit score which will determine whether they have access to loans and also the conditions that come with each loan, which need to suit the borrower.

CHAPTER - 08

Inflation

In this chapter, we will look at:

- ⋙ What inflation is
- ⋙ The role of the Bank of England in controlling inflation
- ⋙ How inflation affects people

Inflation

Inflation is a measure of the rate of rising prices of goods and services in an economy. Inflation can occur when prices rise because of increases in production costs, such as raw materials and wages. We have a finite (limited) number of resources in the world. As we put pressure on these resources by increasing our demands for goods and services, prices rise. An increase in demand for products and services can **cause inflation**, as customers will pay more for the product. **Inflation is the rise in prices over time.**

The online shopping site eBay demonstrates the idea of inflation. The more people who bid for a product and the higher the demand for it, the higher the price for the product. Equally, if no one is interested in the product, it will either not sell or sell for a cheap price.

Question

Can you think of other examples where, because of the limited availability of a product, prices are raised? How about diamonds and other rare jewels? Or even students selling sweets that aren't usually available in the school canteen?

The Bank of England

The Government sets a target inflation rate of 2%, which it deems as reasonable. The Bank of England then tries to meet this target. So whereas a loaf of bread may have cost you £1 previously, it may now cost you £1.02.

Inflation reduces your purchasing power unless you get a pay rise in line with it. Think about it, if inflation rises by 3% your purchasing power is reduced by 3%, which means you can buy 3% less than you used to, with the same salary. However, if your salary rises in line with inflation, then you can buy as much as you did before. If it rises above inflation, then you have greater purchasing power.

In March 2021, it was reported by the national media that nurses were not happy with the planned 1% pay rise in their salaries.

Q: Why might this be?

Q: What does this mean if inflation is rising at 3%?

Q: What is happening to their purchasing power?

Q: Why might nurses be upset?

What if inflation rises quickly and exceeds 2%?

The knock-on effect of inflation rising quickly means people cannot afford to purchase as many items as they used to. If inflation is rising rapidly, the chances are salaries will not keep up with the rises in inflation. So people often start saving rather than buying items, and this can slow down the economy. The lack of buying, as a result, decreases demand for products and services and means many companies can find that sales drop, which then means they have to make redundancies to keep their costs low. This puts further strain on people's income, meaning that they save rather than spend or put off purchasing decisions as they are worried that they may not have work in the future.

Below is a chart that demonstrates what happens when inflation rises quickly. Several questions have been provided to get you thinking. Give them a go!

INFLATION RISES RAPIDLY

What happens to people's purchasing power? Does it grow or decrease?

Do you think people will spend or save at this point? Why?

What happens do the demand for products and services? For instance, people wanting to go to restaurants to eat?

What happens to the number of jobs available as a result? Why?

What happens to consumer spending power as a result?

What if inflation rises rapidly? Answers

ANSWERS

INFLATION RISES RAPIDLY

What happens to people's purchasing power? Does it grow or decrease?

People have lower purchasing power

Do you think people will spend or save at this point? Why?

Save. Because they can do less with their money, they will save for the more important items. For instance, if grocery shopping gets more expensive, they may go out less.

What happens do the demand for products and services? For instance, people wanting to go to restaurants to eat?

It will decrease because people don't have the money to do that anymore

What happens to the number of jobs available as a result? Why?

The jobs available reduces and some companies may make workers redundant due to lack of demand for goods and services

What happens to consumer spending power as a result?

It continues to reduce because they have less money coming in. Whereas a household may have had two incomes, they may now only have one.

Does inflation ever go down?

Yes, this is called deflation. This occasionally happens but rarely in the UK. Small amounts of deflation are OK but not for prolonged periods of time because it is an indicator that people aren't spending money, which can lead to the same problems as above.

So ideally, we want inflation to stay as steady as possible while increasing slowly.

In Summary

Inflation is something all people are affected by. It affects their ability to buy goods and services. The Bank of England tries to control inflation at approximately 2%. Rapid inflation or deflation can have several negative effects on people's everyday lives.

CHAPTER - 09

Investment

In this chapter, we will look at:

- What investment means
- Why people choose to invest
- Some ways people can invest
- The risks and rewards of investments

Investment

Financially, an investment means an asset that is obtained with the intention of allowing it to appreciate in value over time. In simple terms, this is when you put money towards something now, in the hope that it will be worth more in the future.

However, it is important to note that investments can both increase and decrease in value, so investments have an element of risk.

Below, make a list of some things you know you can invest in:

1.
2.
3.
4.

Why people choose to invest

QUESTION

Why do you think people choose to invest rather than just keep the money in a bank account?

1.
2.
3.
4.

People can choose to invest for a variety of reasons. This may include:

- ➲ They want to support a business, artist etc.
- ➲ They want to be part of a business or own particular items that they are investing in

One of the main reasons for investing is depreciation and inflation.

Depreciation: The fall in value of a currency or items
Inflation: The rise in prices over time

You may have heard people older than you complain about how expensive things have gotten compared to when they were younger. Inflation is the rise in prices, and the UK government aims for approximately 2% inflation, which means prices for everyday items are rising by 2% per year. This means that the money you have saved today will buy you less in the future as things will get more expensive.

What does this have to do with investment?

Many people invest because their investment value will grow at a higher rate than inflation. So if they invest £100 in a business that increases its share value by 10%, their money is worth 10% more now, which is more than inflation, so their money is not losing value.

People can invest in a whole host of things. Some of the most common are explained below.

Shares:

Buying a share means you own a stake in a company because once you buy a share, you own part of it. A public company that has shares available on the stock market has a legal responsibility to make its finances available to the public. Companies will make their shares available for people to buy to raise money. This might help them create new products, expand, or take on new projects. If the company performs well, its share value will rise, which means if sold, you can make money from your share.

Let's take an example. If in January 2022 you buy 10 shares in Company X for £5 you have £50 worth of Company X shares. If the company does well in 2022, and by January 2023 their value increases by 10%, making each share worth £5.50, then your total shares are worth £55. And if you sell them, you have made £5. In the same way, if the company performs poorly, its shares may decrease by 10%, for example, and your shares will be worth £45.

This may not seem like a huge amount, but an increase of 10% is likely more than your money would make in the bank, and often people will buy shares in larger quantities to benefit from the increase in value.

In order to invest in this way, you should know about the company you are investing in. One of the most successful investors, Warren Buffet, often states that he only invests in products he understands, such as gum, fizzy drinks, etc., rather than technology or cryptocurrency, which he feels less informed about. Before investing, look at a company's previous performance, and any information about future plans that can help you determine how it may perform in the future. However, as you can imagine, this is pure speculation, and therefore there is an element of risk in this type of investment.

Investing in Index Portfolios

Since many people don't understand individual companies (especially in complex industries they are unfamiliar with, such as pharmaceuticals or mining), they may choose to invest in a portfolio or unit trust. This has a broader category of businesses involved in it, so if a couple of businesses in the portfolio do badly, but others do well, it balances out the performance. The S&P 500 is an example which is an index of the 500 largest US publicly traded companies. They work in a similar way in that you are rewarded or punished depending on the performance of this portfolio of businesses rather than just one business. Therefore, some people argue it is less risky because the risk is spread across several businesses. However, again your investment can both gain or lose value.

Commodities

Some people choose to invest in commodities where the performance of a certain commodity determines the return on investment, for example, gold or oil. Your investment will grow or decline depending on the performance and demand for that commodity.

Property

Also a commodity, some people prefer to invest in property that they may choose to rent out. Much like shares, the value of a property can rise and fall, so for instance, you may buy a house for £180,000, but after a year, its value then drops to £170,000. If renting the property you want to ensure the rent covers mortgage payments. Property also requires maintenance, so spending money on it is necessary before the investor sees returns.

Antiques, Art, and other unique items

Some people may choose to invest in a more unconventional way, choosing to buy artwork that they consider will gain value in the future or other items, such as classic cars. However, these people are often investing in something they feel passionate about and have a great understanding of. For example, early investors in the works of Banksy may have understood that this artist would rise to prominence because they have a passion for art. Other people may have a passion for classic cars and understand that over time, certain cars will rise in value as they become increasingly rare, so purchase them in order to sell them later, either to private buyers or, in the case of art, at auctions held by art galleries. However, it is important to stress that people who invest in these areas often have a real understanding of them and therefore feel like they can invest. Whereas, someone with little or no art knowledge would take a greater risk as they may buy artwork that does not become more valuable.

QUESTION

Why do you think more people choose to invest in shares than they do antiques? Think about the level of knowledge involved in order to make a good investment and thus the level of risk.

In Summary

In this chapter, we have looked at the different reasons for investment and the impact of depreciation on savings. The chapter gives examples of the different types of investments that can be made and highlights that investment can both increase and decrease in value, so always carry an element of risk.

CHAPTER - 10

Insurance

In this chapter, we will look at:

- The meaning of insurance
- The types of insurance available and when it is needed

What is Insurance?

Insurance is a means of protection against financial loss. It protects individuals from unexpected events.

List the different types of insurance that you can get below. If you are not sure, think about the things you would want to protect in case they were damaged.

1.	
2.	
3.	
4.	

What can I get insurance for?

House insurance

There are two types of house insurance; content and buildings insurance. Content insurance protects the possessions inside a house in case they are stolen or damaged due to extreme weather or other risks. Building insurance protects the actual building from damage, such as a fallen roof.

Car insurance

A monthly payment which protects you from damage because of car accidents and medical costs associated with the vehicle collision.

Loss of earnings insurance

Ensures you get a monthly sum if you can't work because of illness over a set period. For example, if a person pays £60 a month in insurance, they may get £2000 per month for up to 2 years if they are ill and unable to work.

Travel insurance

Protects and covers the individual against flight cancellations, loss or theft of expensive items, illness while abroad and ensures you have access to a medical professional, for example.

Pet insurance

Covers medical bills for a pet.

Life insurance

By making monthly instalments, when a person passes away, their family receives a lump sum payout to ensure they are financially stable.

NOTE

In some cases, insurance is compulsory and not a choice. For instance, it is illegal to drive without car insurance.

How does it work?

Monthly or annual payment is made to the insurance company for protection. Should something happen, such as an accident, burglary, etc., depending on the insurance type, the individual can make a claim, get access to medical professionals if they are ill, and be financially supported in line with the details stated in their insurance documents.

Why should you get insurance?

Below is a list of some of the types of insurance you can purchase. Can you think of why, and the things it would protect you against?

There is also a section to highlight when insurance would be needed. For instance, travel insurance is only needed when you have booked travel. Try to complete the below table to the best of your ability, and you can check your answers when finished.

Insurance Type	Why?	When needed?
Travel		
Home - contents		
Home - building		
Life insurance		
Pet insurance		
Income protection insurance		
Health/ Dental Insurance		

A completed table is available below.

Insurance Type	Why?	When needed?
Travel	To protect against any accidents or theft when abroad. Particularly if partaking in extreme sports whilst abroad or travelling with expensive equipment/jewellery. Ensures money is refunded to the customer if flights are cancelled or missed for reasons beyond customers' control.	Only when travelling, although annual travel insurance is available to cover all trips during a year; however, this is likely to be expensive if a person only travels once or twice a year, and it may be cheaper to get insurance each time you travel.
Home - contents	To protect belongings in a house against damage (e.g., because of leaking roof). To protect against burglary/theft.	If renting a property, an individual may choose to get content insurance as the landlord will be expected to have buildings insurance that protects the house itself.
Home - building	To protect the actual house against damage from burst pipes, extreme weather, etc.	When buying a house, the bank will often want to see evidence of buildings insurance before they approve a mortgage.
Life insurance	This ensures that in the event of death, the person's family receives financial support.	Most people get this when they have children to financially support them if anything happens to the parents.
Pet insurance	To cover any veterinary costs	If a person gets a pet
Income protection insurance	To ensure a person has money coming in to pay bills if they can't work due to illness (sometimes other reasons can also be covered).	Most people will get this once they have dependents (family) or when they are more established in their career and have a mortgage (as they don't want to lose their house if they can't work due to illness) as the insurance payments help them pay for their mortgage.
Health/ Dental Insurance	To cover medical bills or dental bills if a person wants to use private practitioners.	Usually as people get older and especially if family members have suffered from medical conditions that may be genetic.

Factors that determine when to get insurance.

Brainstorm some factors that may need to be considered before getting insurance and see how many you can come up with.

1.	
2.	
3.	
4.	

Some factors have been listed below.

- Level of income and if affordable
- Age matters, as you are unlikely to get life insurance at 16, for instance
- Medical history
- Hobbies and activities they take part in and risk level
- Value of belongings a person owns
- Security of job
- Family medical history
- Whether they have pets
- If they have family/dependents
- If they have a mortgage/own a home
- If they have financial support from family/friends
- If they financially support any family/friends
- A person's level of risk that they are happy taking
- Location and whether it is prone to natural disasters
- Access to medical care
- Access to dental care

Factors to consider when buying insurance:

When purchasing insurance, there are numerous factors you need to consider. Some are listed below:

- The amount you need to pay
- If it is a one off or regular payment
- The amount of cover you are getting–so in the case of an event what will be the payout from your insurance company
- The evidence you have to provide
- What are the conditions for insurance–for instance for house insurance the company will often only cover the house if there is an alarm system, locks on all windows, etc.

Is it difficult to get insurance?

It's difficult to get insurance for those who have a poor credit rating. (Credit ratings and how to develop a strong one is covered earlier in this section.) It can also be difficult if a person has a pre-existing health condition and is older as insurance companies class them as more of a risk.

If a person has a history of making insurance claims, this can also make it more difficult for them to get covered by insurance.

However, the above does not mean they cannot get it. Instead, they may just have to pay higher monthly payments.

Does a person get the money back if something bad doesn't happen?

No. Those signing up for insurance are paying for cover in case something bad happens. Also, the insurance company is taking a risk by insuring them as they are likely to pay out more than you have paid in if something terrible happens. So a person does not get their money back but may get a better deal on future insurance deals. For instance, if a person has car insurance and doesn't have an accident, then they may pay less for insurance the following year.

In Summary

We need different types of insurance at different points in our life, for instance when we buy a home, book travel, etc. Factors to be considered before buying insurance are important and reading the details of the insurance policy. Whether one can get insurance is often linked to the level of risk they pose.

CHAPTER - 11

Travelling Abroad

In this chapter, we will look at:

Financial factors to consider when travelling abroad, such as:

- Travel insurance
- Exchange rates
- Different ways to pay for things abroad

Travelling abroad is a time when you can apply many of the principles in this section of the book. For instance, you will have to decide what items you need and want to take with you abroad. You will need to explore the currency of the country you are travelling to and determine how you will pay for things out there. Even if you plan and book everything before you travel, such as getting an all-inclusive hotel, then chances are you will need to bring some money with you for expenses such as taxis, souvenirs, trips, and snacks. Below we will explore the things you need to consider before travelling abroad in more detail.

Travel Insurance:

This is relatively easy to buy online.

Things you must know before buying travelling insurance

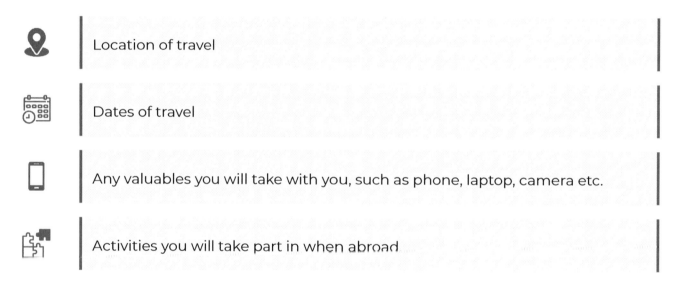

Location of travel

Dates of travel

Any valuables you will take with you, such as phone, laptop, camera etc.

Activities you will take part in when abroad

The amount you pay for travel insurance will be determined on the above factors. Things to consider/look out for when buying travel insurance:

Medical cover:

Probably one of the most important factors of travel insurance. When deciding on a travel insurance provider, consider the service they will provide if you get ill or injure yourself abroad. Will they send you a doctor to your hotel? Cover hospital costs etc., and to what value?

Value of cover for loss of goods:

Does the insurance cover you enough to replace valuable items if they are lost?

Terms of claims:

What do you have to do to make a claim? Is it incredibly difficult? What paperwork will you need to provide, for instance, if your money had been stolen? In many cases, you need to report it to the police and need a police reference number.

Cover for activities:

Particularly good for sports where you could injure yourself, so if you are going on a holiday to ski or climb.

Cover for theft:

If items such as money and passport were stolen, how will you handle this, and how do you go about getting a replacement in the foreign country?

Many comparison websites will compare travel insurance for you, so make sure you check them out before purchasing.

Buying things abroad

There are several ways you can buy things abroad whilst you are on holiday. These are:

- Foreign currency
- Prepaid currency cards
- Debit card
- Credit card
- Traveller's cheques (rarely used and few banks accept them any more)

Things to be mindful of with each of these:

Foreign currency

Before you buy foreign currency (the money the country you are travelling to uses) you will need to check the exchange rate.

Exchange rate

The value of one currency for the purpose of conversion to another.

Different providers will provide you with different exchange rates.

For instance, if you are trying to buy euros to purchase things in France, you will need to see how many euros you can get in exchange for your currency. Please be aware this can vary from provider to provider so you will need to shop around. No matter which method of payments you hope to use, it is always good to carry some foreign currency when travelling so you can pay for things in places where you may not be able to use other forms of payments such as credit cards (e.g., taxis that only accept cash).

Prepaid currency cards

Cards such as Revolut allow you to put money on them (in your own currency) and then exchanges that amount, allowing you to spend that money using the card while abroad. It is important to note you can only spend the money you have on the card and no more. But you can top it up while you are away.

Debit card and credit card

These can often be used abroad; however, please note that most banks will charge for you to use these, and you will need to see what exchange rate they offer. Furthermore, not every shop, café, etc., will accept cards when abroad.

Travellers checks

Rarely used and few banks accept them any more.

Most people will use a mixture of methods to purchase goods and services when they are travelling. For instance, an individual may take 100 euros in cash to pay for snacks while abroad and taxis but then use their credit card for meals, hotel, and any museum tickets.

How do I know how much money I need?

A good way to predict how much money you will need abroad is to look online and do some research before you go. For instance, how much does it cost to eat out in an average restaurant? Many bloggers write about travelling to countries and how much they cost, and all you have to do is search for them online. TUI's holiday spending calculator can also guide you:

https://www.tui.co.uk/holidays/budget-calculator

Phone Charges

If you're travelling abroad, chances are you will be taking your mobile phone along. How much it will cost you to make calls, send messages, or use data will depend on the country you visit. It is worth checking with your phone provider before you go. Phones can be incredibly handy when abroad to help you purchase tickets online for sites you want to visit and help you navigate your way around a new place, or even to have your boarding passes ready for your flight. Therefore, it is a good idea that you are clear about the cost of travelling with a phone. Some phone providers will offer special bundles of data when you travel abroad that are cheaper than merely trying to access data when you get out there.

In Summary

There are several financial factors you need to consider before you go abroad, and we have covered many of them, such as how you wish to pay for things and how you protect yourself should you suffer a theft or an injury while abroad. It is important to put in the work to ensure you have these factors covered before travelling so that you can have peace of mind while you are away.

CHAPTER - 12

Does Money Make You Happy?

In this chapter, we will look at:

- ⋛ The relationship between money and happiness
- ⋛ Some figures which show things such as average salary
- ⋛ The decisions that can be made with money

Have you heard any of the following sayings about money?

"Money doesn't grow on trees"

———————

"Money is the root of all evil"

———————

"The best things in life are free"

———————

Have you heard of any more phrases?

QUESTION - 1

How much money do you think would make you happy once you have a roof over your head and food in the fridge?

QUESTION - 2

What do you think the average salary in the UK is?

QUESTION - 3

How much do you think you would have to earn in order to be earning in the top 5% in the UK?

Statistics:

- The average salary in the UK, according to the Office of National Statistics (ONS) was £25,971 in 2021.
- To be in the top 5% of earners in the UK, you would have to earn £80,000 or more.

When it comes to how much money can make you happy, numerous studies show various amounts, however, looking at these studies collectively, the average appears to be around £43,000–£54,000.

QUESTION - 4

Do any of the above figures surprise you? Did you expect the figures to be higher or lower?

Can we buy happiness?

In 2017, Michael Norton, a professor at Harvard Business School, a prestigious university in the USA, found the following in his research (a summary of his findings is in the TED Talks clip here)

www.ted.com/talks/michael_norton_how_to_buy_happiness?

"Overall, people with more money are generally happier than people with less money. But our research has shown that this relationship is weaker than many people assume.

Saving money is very good for happiness, both now and later.

Investing in others by donating money, for instance, is a large contributor to happiness."

He and his co-researcher came up with 5 principles of spending:

1. Buy experiences
2. Make it a special treat
3. Buy time
4. Pay now, consume later
5. Invest in others

QUESTION - 5

Can you come up with 5 reasons why investing in others may make people happier than spending money on themselves?

1.	
2.	
3.	
4.	
5.	

A few ideas that have been suggested and researched are:

- ➲ It makes people feel useful and positive about themselves.
- ➲ Charities give regular updates to those who donate on the impact their donation is having, which means they may only give once, but get joy from it several times over.
- ➲ Researchers have found it releases a pleasure chemical in our brain, which is also linked to social connection.
- ➲ It makes the person feel generous, so others are nicer to them, which makes them happier.
- ➲ For many people who are religious, it is part of their religion to give to charity (e.g., Islam and Christianity).

QUESTION - 6

Look at the 5 principles of spending that are repeated below. Would you add anything to this list?

1. Buy experiences
2. Make it a special treat
3. Buy time
4. Pay now, consume later
5. Invest in others

In 2014, Forbes magazine found that 84% of millennial employees gave to charity and 70% of them donated more than an hour to a charitable cause. This is higher than previous generations.

Why might that be?

- Think about the role of social media?

- Are young people more aware of the plight of others around the world?

- Think about how social media was used during George Floyd and Black Lives Matter protests.

- What about the impact of sites such as Go Fund Me?

In Summary

Money makes people happy to a certain extent. The choices on how to spend money is just as important as the money itself when it comes to happiness.

CHAPTER - 13

Money and Mental Health

In this chapter, we will look at:

- The mental health impact of money
- Places you can contact to get help

According to the charity Mind, financial stress can lead to physical effects of the body such as depression, lack of sleep, inability to focus, panic attacks, anxiety, and much more. In 2019, the BBC reported that an estimate of 1.5 million people in England were struggling with mental health and debt issues at the same time. [5]

Money and Mental Health is an independent charity committed to breaking the link between financial difficulty and mental health. According to their website, in September 2021 they state "People with mental health problems are three and a half times more likely to be in problem with debt." They also have a wealth of research and a blog on the relationship between money and mental health.

Money can have a profound impact on mental health and vice versa. This may be because of the stress linked to paying off creditors or addictions such as gambling, which leads to a greater mental strain. Traditionally, money has been an area that people have been hesitant to discuss openly, however as it plays such an important part in people's happiness, it is good to see more people openly talking about their finances within reason. (We are not advocating sharing your bank balance with complete strangers or your financial details.)

Below are a series of organisations and their contact details, available at the time of publishing, that offer various support around money and mental health.

The Money Charity offers lots of advice and practical tips on managing finances and stress around money.

https://themoneycharity.org.uk/

Citizens Advice website is a good place to visit as they have debt advisors that can help.

https://www.citizensadvice.org.uk/debt-and-money/

The Debt Advice Foundation provides debt advice and other services to those who are struggling with debt. They also fund and conduct research about the impact of debt on people.

https://www.debtadvicefoundation.org/

Step Change offers free expert debt advice.

https://www.stepchange.org/

---

5   BBC News, Crippling debt 'linked to depression', March 2019,
     https://www.bbc.co.uk/news/business-47693725

GamCare provides a free helpline for anyone suffering with gambling problems and details can be found on their website.

https://www.gamcare.org.uk/

Be Gamble Aware provides a great source of information about the different support options available to those struggling with gambling. Details can be found at

www.begambleaware.org/finding-the-right-support

The NHS also has a support line provided by the Money Advice Service, and they also provide a webchat service and other services that can be found here.

https://www.england.nhs.uk/supporting-our-nhs-people/how-to-guides/financial-wellbeing/financial-wellbeing-support/

The above web page provides a host of links on advice from benefits advice to advice around work and redundancy also. It also has a free budget planner tool and advice for spotting financial scams.

For those suffering financial abuse, Women's Aid and Money Helper offer support and advice. This is available at the following sites:

https://www.womensaid.org.uk/information-support/what-is-domestic-abuse/financial-abuse/

https://www.moneyhelper.org.uk/en/family-and-care/divorce-and-separation/protecting-against-financial-abuse

SECTION - 02

The Economy

WEALTH

TIME ▶

CHAPTER - 01

GDP

In this chapter, we will cover:

- What GDP is
- How it is measured
- Why a country's GDP is important to people
- Drawbacks of focusing on GDP alone

GDP

GDP stands for Gross Domestic Product. This is a monetary measure of the market value of all the final goods and services produced in a specific time period. GDP looks at how much a country is producing (e.g., items, such as tins of beans, or services such as music downloads or educational courses) and their value.

Why might high GDP be important? - GDP is said to be a good indicator of the financial health of a country. Essentially, the more a country trades, the higher its GDP and the wealthier its people should be.

QUESTION

Why would a country want to know how much it is producing and what that is worth? What other factors might it indicate? 'List all the reasons you can think of.

Reasons a country may want to know how much it is trading and things it may indicate
1.
2.
3.
4.

Below is an example of some of the ideas you may have come up with.

- If GDP is growing, it means a country is producing more, which often means more people are in work and have jobs.

- A growing GDP can also show that there will be more jobs in the future for people.

- A shrinking GDP may indicate that a country needs to produce more or invest in new businesses so it can hire people and produce more.

- Often higher GDP means more spending, which indicates how healthy a country's economy is as people are happy to spend money.

- Spending is linked to the standard of living (the way people live), and when GDP is growing, spending is also noted to increase (get better).

- GDP is often a sign of a well-educated/skilled workforce who can contribute skills to the economy and find work.

- High GDP means the government earns more in taxes, which should mean they can provide better public services such as healthcare, the police force, street lighting and road maintenance, and schools.

How is GDP measured?

GDP can be measured in three ways:

Output:

The total value of the goods and services produced by all sectors of the economy—agriculture, manufacturing, energy, construction, the service sector, and government.

Expenditure:

The value of goods and services bought by households and by the government, investment in machinery, and buildings. This also includes the value of exports, minus imports.

Income:

The value of the income generated, mostly in terms of profits and wages.

In the UK, the Office for National Statistics (ONS) publishes one measure of GDP, which is calculated using all three measurements above.

How does GDP impact me?

GDP determines whether we are in a Boom (a period of growth where we are producing more and more goods and services) or a Recession (where we produce less, either because we are not creating what people want or because people don't want to spend.) This affects everyone's life in one way or another.

Brainstorm how high GDP may affect the groups of people listed below.

	Impact
Students leaving college/university	
Person wanting to start a business	
An adult looking for a part-time job to allow them to look after young children	
Government	

Now do the same for low GDP and how it may affect these different groups of people.

	Impact
Students leaving college/university	
Person wanting to start a business	
An adult looking for a part-time job to allow them to look after young children	
Government	

Possible answers have been provided in the following table.

The impact of high GDP

	Impact
Students leaving college/university	As the economy is active and healthy and output is high, it should be easier for young people to find work as more companies will be hiring to help them meet the high demand for their products/services.
Person wanting to start a business	More opportunities to start a business as people are buying goods and services. Think about more cafes opening as more people are at work buying coffee and lunch, for instance.
An adult looking for a part-time job to allow them to look after young children	Easier to find part-time work as businesses are more likely to hire staff to meet production targets and meet the demand of customers.
Government	Fewer people claim financial support as jobs are readily available, therefore more government money can go towards public services rather than financial aid.

The impact of low GDP

	Impact
Students leaving college/university	Harder to find work as people are spending less so there are less job opportunities available as companies are not producing as much
Person wanting to start a business	This can often go either way! People can become fearful of starting a business as people are not buying as many goods and services OR as people cannot find work as easily, they may choose to become self-employed and start their own business. It really depends on the business idea and a person's ability to manage risk.

An adult looking for a part-time job to allow them to look after young children	It may be harder to find flexible work if there are fewer opportunities, but this may depend on industry. For example, some industries may prefer part-time workers if production is low.
Government	More people claim financial aid in order to support themselves as unable to find work. Government funds are directed towards supporting those out of work.

Is GDP the only way to measure the economic health of a country?

Many economists have argued that GDP is a very narrow way to measure the economic health of a nation because it only looks at financial aspects. Further, it is criticised for assuming that high GDP means wealth for the population.

QUESTION

What other factors could be considered when determining the health of a country? What does GDP not tell us? Another way to think about it is, imagine you get off a plane in another country and haven't been told where you are. How do you identify if the country is in a healthy financial state?

Other factors that have been argued to be key indicators of economic health are:

Education:

The theory being that the more educated a population is, the more they can contribute to the economy as the more skilled they are. Thus, high levels of education should lead to growing GDP and a better standard of living.

Health:

The healthier the population, the more people are able to be in the workforce contributing to economic growth.

Alternatives to GDP:

Some economists have argued that a key problem with GDP is that it doesn't actually tell you where wealth lies. For instance, a country could have a very high GDP but still have a sizeable gap between the rich and the poor. Others have argued that we need to look at more than just finances and production, but more human elements.

HDI

The Human Development Index looks at GDP, life expectancy, and education levels. Arguing that this gives a more rounded view of a country's economic health and development.

Gross National Happiness (GNH)

Bhutan was the first country to argue that it would look at factors contributing to the happiness of its population rather than just economic factors. The GNH looks at:

- Living Standards
- Health
- Good Governance
- Ecological Diversity
- Resilience
- Time Use
- Psychological Well-Being
- Cultural Diversity And Resilience
- Community Vitality

This is calculated by 8,000 random households completing a survey. However, it is important to note that trying to measure some of the factors above such as, resilience and well-being, can be very challenging.

a. Make a list of factors below that you think should determine how well a country is doing. For instance, should it just be financial like GDP? Or should we consider more factors, such as the environment?

b. Looking at these factors, how easy are they to measure?

1.
2.
3.
4.

In Summary

This chapter has delved into what GDP is and its impact on people, as well as the advantages of measuring it and its limitations when measuring the development of a country. The chapter has also looked at alternatives to GDP, such as the Human Development Index and Gross National Happiness.

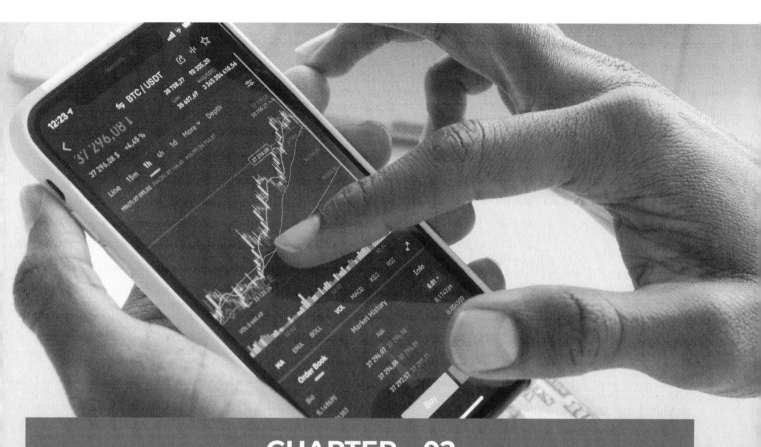

CHAPTER - 02

Free Markets and Supply and Demand

In this chapter, we will look at:

- ⋛ What a free-market economy is
- ⋛ Alternatives to free market economics
- ⋛ Supply and Demand and its role in the free market economy

What is a free market economy?

A free market economy believes that there should be minimum intervention in the market by the government and that independent organisations should provide the goods and services that people need. It believes that the free market can determine what is needed and the price that should be paid. For instance, if a company releases some excellent products that are needed, the demand for those products will grow, and the market will offer the company a fair price because it is a valued product. Moreover, if the product is popular, this will send a signal to other companies that they too should offer it so they will enter the market offering more options and keep prices affordable for customers. Similarly, if the company releases products that the market (people) do not value, the demand for those products will be low and therefore the price will be low. If the demand is really low, few people will buy the product, and eventually the business will have to shut down.

Because of this, free market economists believe that there is no need for the government to enter the market to provide goods or services. As the market will attract businesses that are needed and punish those that do not provide a valued product or service at the market determined price.

Supply and Demand

The free market economy functions on the idea of Supply and Demand.

Supply - The total amount of a specific good or service that is available to consumers.

Demand - Consumer willingness to pay a price for a good or service.

We can see the idea of supply and demand and its impact on the market price through a simple diagram on the right.

What this diagram shows is that if a product enters the market and is supplied (s line), then demand for it will appear (d line) if it meets customer needs and this will set a price for the product (where they meet).

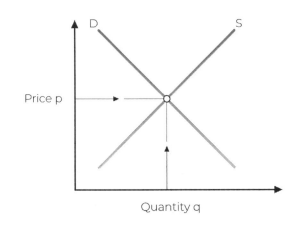

Using the previous diagram, move the demand line to the right, showing demand going up (for example, a product getting more popular). Where does the demand and supply line meet now?

This should show an increase in price from P to P1 and resemble the diagram on the right.

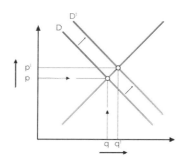

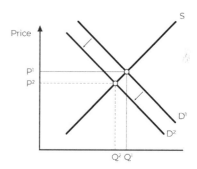

Now do the same if demand was to decrease. What would happen to price in this situation? It should look like the diagram on the right with price going down from P1 to P2.

QUESTION

Can you think of any examples where this may not work?

- ⟳ **For example, where a product is offered/needed and good for the public, but there is little demand for it? (Think about the demand for fruits and vegetables in supermarkets over other convenience products.)**

- ⟳ **Where the market price for a product is set too high for citizens, so the government has to part fund it or provide it themselves (medical care and medication may be an example).**

Drawbacks to the free market economic theory

This theory does have its limits. Customers don't always reward the best products because they may not understand the full benefits of the product or service or be able to afford the market price.

The theory also assumes that businesses can just enter the market and offer their products if they see other businesses being successful in an area. However, supply of a particular good or service may be limited if it is difficult to set up a business in an industry/sector.

Supply

Supply is the total amount of a specific good or service that is available to consumers.

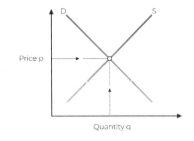

In the image on the right, we go back to the supply and demand model.

Now let's manipulate the supply lines. Imagine a popular product takes off and more and more people start businesses to supply it, so they can benefit from sales of that product and make money.

Draw the Demand and Supply diagram and then add an extra line if supply shifts to the right (increasing). What happens to price? You should see price decrease because now that product is more easily available in the market and the diagram should look like the diagram on the right.

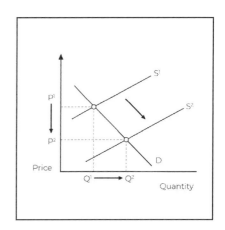

What if businesses can't keep up with making a product or selling it because there is fierce competition or it is too complex to make? The number of suppliers will fall. You can demonstrate that on your diagram by adding a line to the left of the original supply line. This should see prices rise and the diagram should look like the graph on the right:

A shift in supply

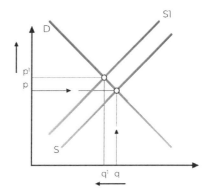

Make a list of companies that are dominant in their field, such as Apple, Microsoft, Google, Amazon, etc. Can you think of any reasons new businesses setting up to compete with them would struggle? The chances are any answers you come up with are known as barriers to entry.

Below are some examples of barriers and some reasons why new businesses may struggle to start up in an industry against existing businesses.

- Less money to spend on marketing.
- Inability to get brand name out to customers.
- Small size at the start may mean inability to offer low prices like the big businesses.
- Legal barriers, such as patents and trademarks.
- High set-up costs of business.
- Supplier agreements. The big companies may have an agreement that suppliers cannot supply competitors.
- Lack of labour supply. Specialists working in an area that you need to recruit from.
- Control over marketing channels. Think about it, many companies advertise through Google, Facebook, etc. How could competitors use them to promote themselves?
- Deals with government for tax breaks that smaller companies won't have.

Alternatives to Free Market Economies

A **command economy** is when government central planners own or control the means of production and determine the distribution of output (basically control the supply of goods and services). To a greater or larger extent, these are visible in Cuba and North Korea.

In Summary

We have looked at how the free market economy works in theory and how it may not work sometimes. This is further explored in the chapter that looks at rational decision-making. The chapter covers supply and demand diagrams and how they can demonstrate what is happening in the market. And finally, an alternative to free market economics.

THE ECONOMY

CHAPTER - 03

The Economic Cycle

In this chapter, we will look at:

- What an economic cycle is
- Factors that determine whether we are in a Boom or Recession
- The impact of a Boom or Recession on people's everyday lives

The **economic cycle** is the fluctuation of the economy between periods of expansion (growth) and contraction (recession). Put simply, it looks at how much a country is trading over time and whether this is increasing or decreasing.

It is often demonstrated with a diagram that looks like this:

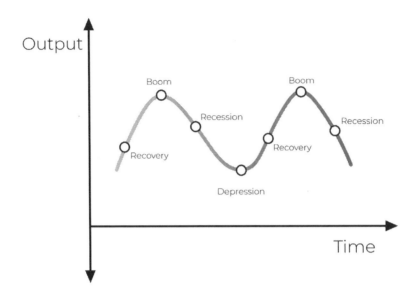

In the previous chapter, we looked at GDP. A boom is when GDP is growing consistently. A recession is when GDP declines for several months.

Confidence

The economic cycle has a lot to do with confidence. The more confident people feel about their finances in the future, the more likely they are to buy things, thus creating more jobs (because someone has to make or provide those goods and services).

Complete the table below on the economic cycle. This looks at what can be expected during the 4 periods of the economic cycle. Questions have been asked in each box for you to answer.

Element of Economic Cycle	GDP	Employment/ Unemployment	Spending habits
Boom	Looking at the previous diagram, is output/GDP high or low?	Do you think this level of GDP will create more or fewer job opportunities? Will there be overtime for workers or redundancies?	Depending on whether it is easy or difficult to find work, will people be spending more or trying to save? Will they be buying luxuries?
Recession	Looking at the diagram, is Output and GDP high or low?	Do you think this level of GDP will create more or fewer job opportunities? Will there be overtime for workers or redundancies?	Depending on whether it is easy or difficult to find work, will people be spending more or trying to save? Will they be buying luxuries?
Depression	Looking at the diagram, is Output and GDP high or low?	Do you think this level of GDP will create more or fewer job opportunities? Will there be overtime for workers or redundancies?	Depending on whether it is easy or difficult to find work, will people be spending more or trying to save? Will they be buying luxuries?
Recovery	Looking at the diagram, is Output and GDP high or low?	Do you think this level of GDP will create more or fewer job opportunities? Will there be overtime for workers or redundancies?	Depending on whether it is easy or difficult to find work, will people be spending more or trying to save? Will they be buying luxuries?

A completed version is below for you to check your answers.

Element of Economic Cycle	GDP	Employment/ Unemployment	Spending habits
Boom	GDP is growing rapidly, which means a country is producing goods and services in high demand.	As a result, there are a lot of job opportunities. It is easy for people to find full or part-time work as businesses need to employ people to keep up with the demand for their product or service.	As more people are employed, households have more income and therefore spending power. As a result, they often spend on luxuries, thus increasing the demand for goods and services even further and growing GDP.
Recession	GDP is declining for several months.	The amount of overtime at work reduces as do job opportunities.	People have less money to spend and fear that they may not have enough to cover their basic needs, so stop spending. This fear can often lead to a depression.
Depression	GDP is declining rapidly and has been doing so for a long time.	High levels of unemployment and redundancies taking place. As a result, the government must provide large levels of financial aid. Many businesses start closing down.	People are scared to spend on luxuries and focus on saving. Often businesses that do best here are low price businesses, such as Poundland, Primark, and supermarkets.
Recovery	GDP grows again, and demand for goods and services grows.	Companies start hiring again. This can often be in just a few industries at first that are benefitting from growth in demand but later benefits others too.	People feel more confident about spending and thus demand for goods and services begin to slowly rise again.

NOTE

*It's important to note that this is a brief outline and quite a simplistic explanation to demonstrate an idea. For instance, certain jobs, goods, and services always remain in demand, such as teachers, doctors, bread, and milk.

Why can't a country just stay in a boom?

Booms often lead to inflation because there are a finite number of resources and the increased demand for these (due to people having more spending money) pushes prices up. This eventually means that people cannot afford goods/services and therefore reduces demand, which then impacts GDP by lowering it. This is similar to when lots of people bid for something on eBay, the price goes up, and eventually people stop bidding when bidding reaches a price they no longer want to pay.

Booms can also lead to excessive borrowing. As people's desire to buy goods and services continues to grow, people often borrow money to purchase these goods/services. When the population has to repay this borrowed money, spending slows down, thus lowering GDP.

How do we get out of a recession/depression?

QUESTION

Think about how we could encourage large groups of people to spend. What could be done by the government or the banks? What could businesses do?

1.	
2.	
3.	
4.	

Some answers to the above are listed below:

The government often steps in to manage a recession and help a country stabilise. Below are some things that are done, also known as Government Intervention.

Government intervention

There are several actions that governments will take in order to aid a country's recovery. Some of these are below:

Government spending into public services

Governments will often spend on public services, such as building projects and roadworks in order to support jobs and industry.

Government support of businesses

Funding and supporting new businesses or those that exist to ensure people stay in work.

Winning of contracts or projects

The 2012 Olympics was seen by some as a huge win for the British economy in the long term. It attracted tourism and investment into infrastructure, which created jobs and an influx of money. It not only created work and encouraged spending locally, but also brought in a lot of foreign trade through tourism.

Investment in retraining and education

Training schemes, funding of courses, and apprenticeship schemes is a way of ensuring the country has the skills to start businesses and invest in industries that are needed and whose products and services are needed globally.

The importance of foreign trade

One way a country can ensure it doesn't rely too much on local spending is by encouraging foreign trade. So, if people are limiting their spending locally products can still be sold abroad, maintaining jobs.

Entrepreneurship and attracting businesses

The economy relies on businesses creating products and services that are in high demand. They then go on to create jobs and wealth. Governments can put in place schemes that allow businesses to start up by providing mentorship or financial incentives. Schemes for introducing businesses to foreign markets and holding international trade fairs allow businesses to increase demand overseas, meaning that businesses don't just rely on local demand.

In Summary

We have looked at the cyclical nature of the economy and how GDP/Output affects the economy, jobs, and spending confidence. The impact of booms and recessions on peoples' lives has also been covered. Finally, this chapter has also mentioned some steps the government takes in order to manage the economy and ensure some stability.

CHAPTER - 04

The Assumption of Rational Decision-Making

This chapter, we will look at:

- ⋛ What rational decision-making is
- ⋛ How economic theory is based on it
- ⋛ Alternatives to rational decision-making
- ⋛ Why you should think about rational decision-making

Rational decision-making assumes that individuals **always** make decisions that provide them with the highest amount of personal utility (total satisfaction received from consuming a good or service). These decisions provide people with the greatest benefit or satisfaction, given the choices available. Based on this theory, economists assume certain behaviours will take place. Examples of this are:

- Customers will always buy the best product available on the market that will give them the most benefits.

- People will always start and run businesses with the goal to maximise the profit they make. Rational decision-making helps economists make predictions about things like: How people will react to government intervention, the creation of new products, services, and industries, and even the supply and demand graphs we have looked at make assumptions about human economic behaviour. Rational decision-making is based on certain assumptions. These are:

    1. The customer has access to all the information necessary to make the best decision and understands the information.

    2. They know exactly what they are looking for and how it will make them happy.

    3. They are aware of all the alternatives to the product they are buying.

    4. They have the time and resources to compare all the products available on the market to make sure they buy the one that will make them the happiest.

Using the 4 assumptions above, think about instances when they may not be true. There are some hints in the next table provided.

Rational decision-making assumption	Example of when this might not be true
1. The customer has access to all the information necessary and understands it to make the best decision.	Does a customer need to know everything about a car before they purchase? Is it possible for us to have ALL the information about a product and understand it before we purchase every item?
2. The customer knows exactly what they are looking for and how it will make them happy.	Have you ever made a purchase on a whim? Did you always calculate the happiness it would bring you? Can you think of items you buy in an emergency without calculating all the benefits?
3. The customer is aware of all the alternatives to the product they are buying.	What was the last item you bought? Before buying it, did you research every other product out there that was similar?
4. The customers have the time and resources to compare all the products available on the market to make sure they buy the one that will make them the happiest.	Linked to the above, if we researched all items when buying a watch or a t-shirt, for example, we would not have the time to do much else.

Some responses and examples to the above are provided below:

Rational decision-making assumption	Example of when this might not be true
1. The customer has access to all the information necessary and understands it to make the best decision.	Think of situations where we trust professionals for their expertise and advice. For example, medical procedures, when hiring plumbers, builders, or even buying a car or going to get our car fixed. In these situations, the professional (doctor, plumber, builder, mechanic) knows more than us, and we trust them to charge a fair price. Customers may even be given the information but not understand it. Think about your TV. Just because you have the manual doesn't mean you read it or understand what every button does.
2. The customer knows exactly what they are looking for and how it will make them happy.	Think of situations where people buy items they were not anticipating buying or cannot calculate their value. For example, impulse buys are often made last minute. We do not rationally calculate what we are looking for from the item (this could be trainers or clothes we see in a shop window, for instance). And we will pay the price to make ourselves happy in that instance. Another example may be for people buying something for the first time, such as a car or house, and they may not be aware of how happy that item may make them in the future.
3. The customer is aware of all the alternatives to the product they are buying.	What was the last item you bought? Before buying it, did you research every other product out there that was similar? Probably not. You may have researched the top three but definitely not every single item; otherwise, you may never have got around to buying it! Items that need to be bought in an emergency also will be purchased without alternatives being researched, such as when washing machines or other electrical items have to be replaced in a hurry.

Rational decision-making assumption	Example of when this might not be true
4. The customers have the time and resources to compare all the products available on the market to make sure they buy the one that will make them the happiest.	Linked to the above, if we researched all possible items when buying a watch or a t-shirt, for example, we would not have the time to do much else. Again, this assumes that the customer has a detailed understanding of a product. When buying a phone, the most likely things people will compare are price, functionality, the package, and the look of the phone rather than all the technical details as they may not understand them or have the time.

QUESTION

Think about all the factors that influence your choices when buying a pair of trainers.

Your list may include things like:

- ⮐ Advertising
- ⮐ Affordability
- ⮐ Style of the trainer
- ⮐ Availability - whether it is in stock when we go shopping
- ⮐ Recommendations/Reviews

Some alternatives to rational decision-making as a customer

Heuristics/Anchoring

Based on the idea that we use shortcuts to make decisions, such as what is quickly available and the cheapest option.

Herd Mentality

We decide based on the decisions others have made and are influenced by others.

Altruism

We can decide based on what will create the greatest good for other people. Think about donations to charity or those who buy items that may not be the best on the market but help a cause.

Habit

Some purchases are made out of habit or what we are used to. For instance, if someone is used to having a specific brand of toothpaste when they live with their parents, they are likely to continue to buy that brand as they get older.

Regret aversion

Sometimes we buy to avoid regret later, therefore, taking advantage of a deal or promotion to avoid regret of missing out on it. Think about sale shopping. Often people don't need the item being bought but have seen it at a discounted price and want to avoid regretting not getting that item later.

Rational decision-making and business

Applying the rational decision making theory to business means that businesses will always try to keep costs as low as possible for the greatest profit. But again we know this is not always true. Of course, profit is important for the business to survive but it is not always the reason businesses start or the primary reason why they function. In fact, in 2016, The Financial Times ran an article stating that 'Companies with a purpose beyond profit tend to make more money.'

[6]In fact many companies such as AirBnB didn't make any profit for several years.

QUESTION

Do you know of any businesses that did not have profit as their major driving force when they first started?

Body Shop	**Google**	**Facebook**	**Tesla**
One of the first retailers to promote the ideas of fair trade in cosmetics and the environmental impact of the cosmetics industry	Started as a PHD project	Started as a university site	Originated to prove that a fast stylish environmentally friendly car is a possibility

Activity - 2

Make a list of any other benefits a company and its owner may get from starting a business other than profit?

1.
2.
3.
4.

6   Financial times, Companies with a purpose beyond profit tend to make more money, https://www.ft.com/content/b22933e0-b618-11e5-b147-e5e5bba42e51

Some have been listed below:

- Making a positive impact on society
- Making a positive impact on the environment
- They may enjoy problem-solving
- Working for oneself
- Employing people and giving job opportunities
- Promoting human rights
- As a way of promoting their creative work
- Freedom in managing their day and working around other commitments

Why should I care about rational decision-making?

The economic models we look at in this book and that form the basis of economics and economic policies are based on rational decision-making. Such as the supply and demand models, which assume if an excellent product is released, people will want it, for example.

As a *consumer*, it gives you something to think about when making purchases in the market. Consider your motivations. Are you making a purchase due to herd behaviour? Have you genuinely researched your product to gain maximum benefits? Or are you happy getting something because it is popular?

As a potential business owner or when working in a business – Ask yourself, do customers know all the benefits of the goods and services you are providing? How are they affected by their peers? How could your business utilise herd behaviour?

In Summary

This chapter has covered what rational decision-making is and the assumptions it is based on. We have explored where these assumptions may not hold true seeing the limitations of rational decision-making and then identifying some alternatives.

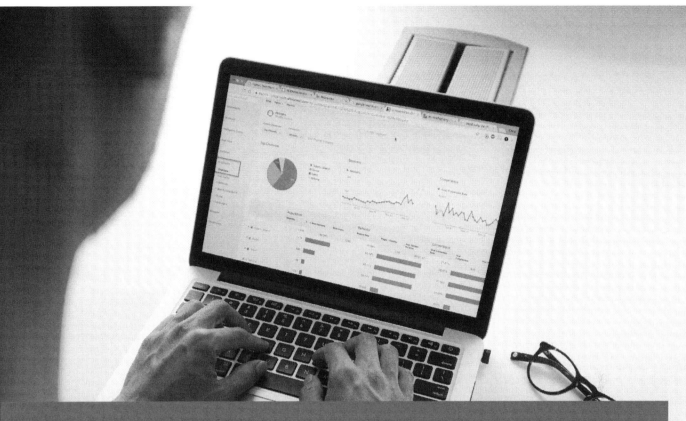

CHAPTER - 05

Disposable Income

In this chapter, we will cover:

> What disposable income is

> How it is affected by inflation

> Disposable income and the relationship with interest rates

> Why disposable income is important to everyone

Disposable income

Disposable income is the money left after taxes are paid. This money is available to be spent or saved as one wishes.

Often the higher the disposable income for the population, the wealthier a nation is.

Higher disposable income can often lead to economic growth as people have more money to buy goods and services. This means more goods and services need to be produced and offered, therefore creating more jobs.

In general, people want their disposable income to be high so that they have more money to spend.

How are disposable income and inflation related?

Inflation is a general increase in prices and fall in the purchasing value of money.

Because we have finite (limited) resources, the more people who want a good or service, the higher its value has become. Think about diamonds. They are expensive because they are rare. Similarly, if you ever go on eBay, the more people who bid for an item, the higher the price gets, because there are a few products that can be produced. Thus, if the general population has a high disposable income, the demand for goods and services rises as do prices, leading to inflation.

The UK Government sets the inflation rate at 2% to keep it steady.

QUESTION

Why would the government try to control inflation (the rate at which prices are rising?). Think about how a higher inflation rate might affect people on different wages?

How the government controls inflation

One way that the government can stop inflation from rising and people from spending is by increasing the interest rate.

Interest is the cost for borrowing money (the additional amount that needs to be paid back when money is borrowed) and the reward for saving (the additional amount that the bank will give you for saving with them).

QUESTION

How will an increase in interest rate impact inflation? Think about whether people will choose to spend or save?

If the government charges more for loans, then people will reduce their borrowing and thus their spending. If they increase the interest paid on saving, more people will use their disposable income to save rather than spend. Therefore, the number of goods/services demanded will fall, as will prices, reducing inflation.

By raising interest rates, the government ensures that people want to save (because they will get a higher interest on their savings). Therefore, helping to control inflation.

Maximising your disposable income

There are several ways to maximise your disposable income and thus buying power.

1. Manage your costs - Most people will do this as a first attempt to manage their disposable income. Shopping around to get the best internet gas and electricity deals allows people to keep their costs low and more money to be spent on other purchases.
2. Gain another source of income - Such as an additional job or side hustle (see "Side Hustle" chapter)
3. Work towards pay rises - This will allow a greater level of income and should increase disposable income, depending on whether or not taxes increase.
4. Develop skills that are sought after in the marketplace to gain higher paid employment or seek payment to help others develop those skills.

In Summary

Disposable income plays an important part in the standard of living for most people. This chapter has looked at how disposable income is affected by interest rates and some methods to increase disposable income.

CHAPTER - 06

Taxes

By the end of this chapter, students will know:

- What taxes are
- The kinds of taxes that exist
- Where taxes are spent by the government

There is the old idiom that only two things are guaranteed in life, and they are death and taxes. So, let's talk about taxes.

Taxes

Taxes are a compulsory contribution to state revenue, levied by the government on workers' income and business profits or added to the cost of some goods, services, and transactions.

So, to be clear, people pay taxes via their salaries, through their businesses if they own one, and on products that they buy. The first £12570 is not taxed.

How much do we pay in tax?

At the time of writing in 2021, there are three income tax rates: 20%, 40%, and 45%. The amount of tax you pay depends on how much you earn. Someone on the median national salary of £30,800, paying the 20% basic rate of tax, can expect to see £616 disappear from their monthly pay packet in income tax and national insurance contributions. Earn more and you will see an even bigger percentage taken out. Someone on £80,000 a year, paying 40% tax on part of their earnings, will see a monthly deduction from HM Revenue & Customs of £2,080.

What types of taxes are there?

There are many taxes, including income tax, national Insurance, VAT (value-added tax), stamp duty, inheritance tax, capital gains tax, fuel duty, etc.

Why do we pay taxes?

Legal argument

Paying your taxes is a legal responsibility as an adult in the UK, and therefore failing to pay taxes or pay the correct amount can result in a criminal conviction

Moral argument

Remember the free market. Well, one issue is it forgets the interconnectivity of individuals. Yes, in theory, people should be able to pay for the things they need, but who pays for the services that we all need? Like streetlights? The sewage system that ensures there isn't the spread of a disease like we have seen in the past? Even though you might not drive, you rely on good roads getting your food to supermarkets or that Amazon delivery you may be waiting for this evening! Taxes pay for these. Another moral argument might be that if we do not collect money for taxes we would be less able to support those more vulnerable in society needing government support.

- Legal System
- Forestry
- Culture
- Housing benefit
- Defence
- Social Services
- Overseas Aid
- Public Prisons
- NHS
- Education
- Disability Benefit
- Environment
- Pensions
- Flood Defence Systems
- Food Standards Agency

Taxes go towards these public goods and the NHS, which saw the treatment of victims of the COVID-19 virus, they fund research into areas, such as cures for cancer and HIV, and they ensure that our elderly are looked after. They fund the school system, the legal system, and much of the public transport system. Without which the country would struggle.

Obviously, with a government body that oversees extensive areas with such a large volume of public money (estimated at over £850bn in 2021), there is waste. This can often be in the form of bureaucracy (often paperwork to sign off things that require public money).

The chart available at:

http://image.guardian.co.uk/sys-files/Guardian/
documents/2008/09/12/13.09.08.Public.spending.pdf

shows government spending in 2007/2008. Although quite out of date, it shows proportionally where the bulk of public taxes go and their proportion.

Have a look at the chart above. If not available, the government website often highlights public spending as a tax summary.

https://www.gov.uk/government/publications/how-public-spending-was-calculated-in-your-tax-summary/how-public-spending-was-calculated-in-your-tax-summary

Are you surprised by the volume of spending and how it was assigned? For instance, did you expect so much money to go towards defence? Or paying back interest on the national debt?

If you handled the public budget, how would you assign money? What would make up the top 10 things you would spend public money on?

1.	
2.	
3.	
4.	
5.	
6.	
7.	
8.	
9.	
10.	

Commercial Taxes

So far, we have spoken about personal taxes, but there are also commercial taxes. These come from businesses or property purchases, for example.

I've heard some businesses avoid taxes?

Some businesses avoid taxes by registering in countries that have lower tax rates. Although this is legal, it is unethical.

QUESTION

Why might people be upset and protest if a company is avoiding paying taxes?

Below are some reasons, although these are not extensive:

Lack of contribution to society

Companies use public services and what taxpayers' money contributes towards. This might be the roads and benefitting from quick delivery times, for instance, or the public sewage system that the government maintains. Therefore, it seems unfair that they don't always contribute to the pot of money that provides those goods.

Fear of higher taxes

The country needs a certain amount of money in order to provide public services. There is the fear that by not contributing, companies lead to higher tax rates for residents because the government needs the money.

Fear of cutting services

Without taxes, the government cannot continue to provide services particularly to the very poor. This is a sensitive point when it comes to the NHS, which treats all patients whatever their background.

In Summary

We have looked at the range of taxes that people may pay during their lifetime and where the government spends those taxes. We have also discussed how some businesses may avoid paying taxes and why this can lead to protests against that business.

SECTION - 03

The World of Work

CHAPTER - 01

The Workplace, Sectors, and Industry

In this chapter, we will look at:

- ⇝ The difference between Industries and Sectors
- ⇝ The largest industries in the UK and why you should know about them
- ⇝ The workplace and different working environments/structures
- ⇝ What the changing workplace means for young people when they enter it

Industry and Sectors

An industry is a group of companies that are related based on their primary business activities. In modern economies, there are dozens of industry classifications. Industry classifications are typically grouped into larger categories, called sectors.

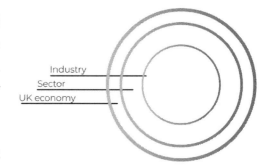

Sectors represent a large segment of an economy that includes many companies and is broader than industry. For example, travel, security, and car leasing.

In 2021, the ten biggest industries by revenue, according to IBIS world[7] in the UK, were:

🛒	Supermarkets
	Pension funding
	Construction contractors
🏛	Banks
🚗	New car and light motor vehicle dealers
🏥	Hospitals
	General insurance

---

7   IBIS World, Biggest Industries by Revenue in the UK in 2021 - https://www.ibisworld.com/united-kingdom/industry-trends/biggest-industries-by-revenue/

Management consultants

Pharmaceutical wholesaling

Computer consultants

This may have been affected by the pandemic, with many retail businesses and restaurants closed. Therefore, it is no surprise that their revenue figures would have suffered. Therefore, if we do a quick search for the biggest industries in the UK for 2019, before the COVID-19 pandemic struck the UK, we see that others, such as tourism, agriculture, manufacturing, and Food and Drink, feature in the top 10 as well.

Conduct online research. Look at a list of industries by typing in "Industries in the UK". Pick 5 that you are unsure of. List the industry and what they do in the table below. Then research the jobs they offer.

Industry	What organisations in this industry do	The types of jobs they recruit for

Why should this interest young people?

Industries need talent, which refers to the people who have the skills required by the industry to be successful. Therefore, for future job prospects, it is good to know the industries that are large in your country as they will look for talent. It can also help you identify industries that are growing and may become dominant in the future, providing work opportunities. Or shrinking, thus having fewer job opportunities. Engineering is an industry that is growing in prominence and is always trying to recruit individuals with talent.

It is important to understand that different industries grow and shrink depending on the resources available to them (funding, talent and skills of the population, access to resources, and alternatives available in the market.) In the 1980s, for instance, we saw the mining industry disappear because of developments in cleaner energy, government actions, and other factors.

The workplace

Workplace is a place where people work, such as an office, factory, farm, shop etc.

The workplace is also changing, particularly after the pandemic, which saw millions of people shift to working from home. There has been much debate as to whether there is any reason to return to the old way of working that usually involves travelling to a place of work.

List in the table below the advantages and disadvantages of working from home and working in a traditional working environment. Try to think about how the choice between working from home would affect the social and family life of workers.

Working in a traditional workplace such as office/factory		Working from home	
Advantages	**Disadvantages**	**Advantages**	**Disadvantages**

A table with advantages and disadvantages has been provided. Check it against your own list of advantages and disadvantages to see if there is anything you did not consider.

Working in a traditional workplace such as office/factory		Working from home	
Advantages	**Disadvantages**	**Advantages**	**Disadvantages**
Teamwork with other members of staff.	Time taken to travel to and from work is wasted and costly.	Flexibility of working around other commitments such as school drop-offs and pick-ups.	Worst work-life balance, as some people argue that their space for relaxing is associated with the high stress of work, meaning they don't switch off.
Build a social circle.	Lack of flexibility of working hours, usually 9 am-5 pm.	Don't spend time/ money commuting from and to work.	From a management point of view, it may be harder to manage a team you don't see face to face often. Further, managers may struggle to oversee work completed by their staff, and they may not catch mistakes until it is too late.
Access to equipment.	Can be distracting, particularly in open-plan offices, not allowing for detailed work and concentration over long periods of time.	Some people argue it allows for better work-life balance as employees can complete other commitments around work.	Building team relationships and camaraderie is harder, as people are not physically present.

| Working in a traditional workplace such as office/factory | | Working from home | |
Advantages	Disadvantages	Advantages	Disadvantages
Sharing of ideas and best practices happens more naturally as people talk when in the office together.		From a business point of view, the cost of running an office/workplace is greatly reduced as do not need desks for all staff if staff only come in when they need to or not at all.	Impact on social life: As people get older, they rely on more work environments to socialise and make friends. If working from home, this may not happen.
Purpose-built work environment, and for some businesses, working from home is not a possibility, for example, retail.		Some people can focus better at home.	

QUESTIONS

a. What would you prefer, working from home or working in the office?

b. Do you think people's preferences are likely to change with age? Why? Why not?

c. Many companies are proposing a mixed approach by allowing people to come into the office a few times a week, for instance, and letting them work from home the rest of the time. Do you think this would be the best approach? Why? Why not?

The changing forms of employment in the workplace

The workplace is seeing a growth in the number of businesses relying on a contingent workforce. This means they rely on intermittent or consultant employees. These employees focus on projects and bring their expertise and skills to a project or a problem in order to help a business, and work on a project for a period of time rather than as permanent employees of a company. Once the project is complete they are either asked to stay on for another project or let go. For example, to develop a company website and strong online presence, a business has three options:

1. Have their own permanent employees complete the work and always focus on the online elements of the business.
2. Outsource to an agency that specialises in this area and pay them for the work they do as a project or monthly fee to maintain an online presence.
3. Hire independent contractor(s) to work on the project, get it up and running, and hand it over to staff in the business when they are done.

Options 2 and 3 are being increasingly used by businesses. There are several reasons for this. This method of employing staff can be cheaper and helps businesses control costs. Some businesses also argue that they get to use specialists for certain projects this way who may cost a lot if they were hired permanently but the business can benefit from them on a short term basis.

What does this mean for young people?

Recent statistics by the ONS and business magazines have found that young people are changing jobs every 2 years, which considering the above move to contingency staffing is not a surprise as they are more likely to work on projects. This means in order to prosper in the workplace, focusing on a niche skill is becoming ever more important while being aware of the larger industry. This is called specialisation.

Specialisation

Specialisation is the process of concentrating on and becoming an expert in a particular subject or skill.

Specialisation is not only beneficial to those doing project-based work but more permanent employees too. For instance, journalists who specialise in particular areas (foreign affairs in India specifically or a particular sport for example) are likely to know more about the history of that area and provide more valuable content such as articles/blogs and thus gain a greater following and better employment opportunities. Another example might be an individual in IT who focuses on security issues for high street banks. That expertise will become valuable over time and something they can demand a higher wage for.

Young people will struggle to specialise as soon as they enter the workplace, as they will need to get a broad understanding of the industry they are in. However, as they develop in their career, they will often look for areas they wish to focus on in order to be the "go-to person" for that niche.

Don't forget the average person is likely to have several jobs and career changes (or at least want to) throughout their working life.[8] Some estimates suggest that those leaving school now will have approximately 5 different careers during their working life; therefore, someone can change specialisms over time and branch out after really mastering one area.[9]

In Summary

This chapter has identified the difference between sectors and industry and highlighted the importance of having knowledge of dominant industries. It has also outlined the changing nature of the workplace, considering the pros and cons of working from home and in traditional settings. Finally, it highlights the shift in employment patterns from permanent employment to more project-based employment and what that means for young people.

8   Office of National Statistics, Analysis of Job changers and stayers - https://www.ons.gov.uk/economy/nationalaccounts/uksectoraccounts/compendium/economicreview/april2019/analysisofjobchangersandstayers

9   Careers in Depth, The current state of career change in the UK, https://www.careersindepth.com/post/the-current-state-of-career-change-in-the-uk

CHAPTER - 02

Recruitment

In this chapter, we will look at:

- How recruitment is changing and may continue to change
- Identify what this means for young people entering the workplace
- How young people can best prepare for the new way in which companies recruit
- How to manage your online presence to help with job searching

Recruitment

The recruitment process is something people have to go through when looking for work, and it is changing. Below you can see the traditional route vs. the route that is taking shape.

Traditional Recruitment Route

1. Company realises they have a vacant post
2. Draw up Job Description (JD) and Person Specification (PS), which highlights what the person needs to do and any required qualifications
3. Advertise post internally and/or externally
4. Person looking for work sees the job advertised and applies if suitable for them
5. The company checks applicants against JD and PS and shortlists those they want to interview
6. Interview process takes place to select a candidate for the job
7. The job is offered to the suitable candidate if there is one
8. If the candidate accepts, they are trained to do well in the company throughout their time there

Think about the recruitment process above. For each stage, consider whether it is the best way to recruit a person. Some things to think about are listed below.

➲ *Could any of these steps be missed?* For instance, the cost of advertising a post, which is often expensive, could be avoided if they simply asked current employees to recommend people or if senior staff had a network of professionals they knew and could recruit from. Many industries already recruit based on recommendations, such as Law, Accountancy etc.

- *Why might it be a bad idea to draw up a Job description before meeting a person? Could there be benefits to meeting them first and drawing it up with the potential candidate to play to their strengths?*

- *Does an interview really tell you what a person is like?* Why? Why not? You could research the pros and cons of interviews on Google. Think about whether they give the candidate an opportunity to be their true selves. How do some people perform under pressure? How does the company check that what the candidate is saying is true?

Although the above traditional recruitment method is likely to still take place in many professions, especially for roles that recruit those who are just starting in their careers and have limited experience. Changes are occurring in the way people are recruited, particularly later on in their career.

Alternative Recruitment Method

1. A company could realise it has a post available or always look out for talented individuals with a particular skill set (e.g., lawyers to join a firm or engineers).

2. Look for individuals with those skills through networks, colleagues, or online through recruitment sites, personal blogs, and online portfolios.

3. Ask suitable individuals to come in for a chat about their experience and speak to them about projects the company is currently undertaking and likely to be working on in the future.

4. Discuss how the individual could contribute to the business.

5. Decide whether to create/offer the individual a position.

This more flexible method of recruitment means that companies won't always advertise posts but will be constantly looking for talent to hire. As a result, an individual's online presence will become increasingly important as well as their reputation among people they work with.

What are the advantages of this method over the previous one? I've asked some questions below to help you.

- ➲ Why might an informal discussion be a better method of understanding what a potential employee is like than an interview? Think about nerves and the benefits of speaking to someone in a more relaxed setting.
- ➲ Why might waiting to see what the strengths of an individual are before drawing up a Job Description help a company?
- ➲ However, could this mean the company may struggle to fill all its skills gaps if it doesn't decide what it needs people to do first?
- ➲ Would a young student be successful during this type of recruitment method if they had never had a job before? Why? Why not?

New Ways of Recruitment

Below are a few other things to look out for, in the way recruitment is changing:

1. Initial interview with chatbots that can eliminate people based on their answers (especially useful for companies who get a high number of applicants per post).
2. COVID-19 has already seen a rise in video interviews, and this is likely to continue.
3. Using social media to recruit, particularly for creatives who show their work online. Journalists have been hired after editors have read their blogs as they know they will bring an audience with them to the paper. (Please see the "Side Hustle" chapter for more information about this.)

Managing Your Online Presence

Your online presence is likely to become ever more important during the recruitment process, giving recruiters the opportunity to learn more about you.

Below are some of the online sites that a recruiter may use to learn more about a potential employee. Think about what your online presence through these channels shows.

- Facebook
- Snapchat
- TikTok
- Instagram
- Fundraising websites. If you have ever fundraised for charity, this information is often available online (e.g., just giving pages are often live for many years after a fundraising event).
- Blogs/websites you have started or you may have contributed to.
- Reviews left for hotels/restaurants etc..
- Online videos referencing you

QUESTION

How can you manage your online presence positively? Is there room to make your online presence stronger?

Some key things you can do to manage your online presence have been listed below.

1. Make sure you have managed your privacy settings on each of the social media channels so that things you want to be private are only shown to those you connect with/approve.

2. Keep things positive. Posting about things/people you dislike does not portray you in a positive light. Of course, if you are talking against an injustice such as child labour, then make sure you are informed before posting.

3. Avoid profanity. You will struggle to find employment if your employer finds a series of videos online of you swearing at people. Think about the impression you want to make.

4. Keep private things private. Most people have a personal life and professional life. It is important to keep the two separate. Be mindful of what you share on social media.

5. Be careful who you engage with. Both for your own safety and to protect your reputation. You do not want to do a series of videos with someone about something you love (e.g. computer games), and then later realise they hold racist views that they share online. This can tarnish your reputation by association.

Using the internet to help you find work in the future

An individual's online presence can be powerful and the internet can be used in empowering ways to help young people find work. Again, some examples have been listed below, but many more are available.

1. Showcase your talent. If you want to sing, this may be through TikTok or Instagram. If you are an artist, you may set up a Pinterest board. If you want to write, you could start by blogging. Or even have your own website to showcase your talent. You can then make the link available to people you want to be able to see it.

2. Set up an online CV to highlight your achievements. Sites such as LinkedIn are online CV platforms for people.

3. Research companies you would like to work for and reach out to them for work experience. If they cannot accommodate this, you could request a short chat with the person who works in your dream profession and ask questions about their job, their work history, how they got to the position they are in now, and what their typical day looks like.

4. Look at what other people who are in the profession are doing. Do these things interest you? How can they inspire you to develop your own talents?

How can young people better equip themselves for the recruitment process?

The challenging thing for young people is to confidently present themselves at interviews. To do this, you need to know about the role you are applying for and be able to talk about it with confidence. Some ways to do this are:

1. **Read job descriptions.** These are readily available online and include job breakdowns and what a person does in them. Go on to any recruitment website, such as Indeed or Total Jobs, and you'll find a breakdown of jobs and what people in those jobs are required to do.

2. **Ask for work experience.** Ask to go in for a set period of time and help answer phones, make coffee, and just try to understand the business.

3. **Shadow a professional.** If work experience isn't possible, ask to shadow a person doing the job you want for just one day or ask to have just a half-hour chat with them about their role.

4. **Read blogs or follow peoples' profiles online.** Look at what people who are fantastic at what you are looking to do are doing, in terms of their professional achievements. This will give you the ability to talk about your aspirations.

5. **Keep updated on new projects.** If you want to enter the gaming industry, make sure you are aware of the latest games that have come out and how they have performed. If you like architecture, research the newest building in your city or further afield and decide what you like/dislike about them. This will develop your ability to have an opinion and give you something to discuss at the interview.

In Summary

The way companies are recruiting is changing and becoming more creative with the use of technology. As a result, those looking for work need to be mindful of their online presence and proactively present themselves in a positive light and with an active interest in the field they hope to be recruited in. Yet, these changes also present opportunities for people to be better prepared for these roles and the recruitment process as a whole.

Note: Please note that you must stay safe when asking to shadow people or go on work experience. Look for larger firms rather than individuals and never put yourself in danger. Always tell someone where you will be and discuss your work experience opportunities with your parents/guardian.

CHAPTER - 03

The Side Hustle

In this chapter, we will look at:

- What a side hustle is
- The move to creating several sources of income
- Some ideas on how to develop a side hustle for the future

According to the IPSE, the UK had 4.4 million solo self-employed people,[10] meaning they work for themselves and do not employ people. We may know them as freelancers who offer a particular set of skills, such as graphic design. In addition to this, in January 2021, *Micro Biz Mag* magazine offered the below statistics about the number of people with a side hustle as well as their primary job.

- ⮑ There are 1.1 million people in the UK with a second job or who are self-employed in addition to a primary job.
- ⮑ That's 3% of the working population.
- ⮑ Despite this, 25% of people in the UK claim to have a side hustle.
- ⮑ 37% of people in the UK say that their salary alone does not allow them to have a comfortable lifestyle.

These changes have led to growth in the gig economy.

Gig Economy

A labour market characterised by the prevalence of short-term contracts or freelance work as opposed to permanent jobs.

What is a Side Hustle?

A piece of work or a job that you get paid for in addition to doing your primary job.

Make a list of the reasons someone would want to do additional work that would earn them some money on the side along with their primary job.

---

10   IPSE, https://www.ipse.co.uk/policy/research/the-self-employed-landscape/the-self-employed-landscape-report-2020.html

Reasons someone would want to do additional work to their primary job:

1.	
2.	
3.	
4.	

Some answers have been provided here:

- ⮑ Allows some people to pursue a more creative life that they may not explore at work. For instance, an accountant may enjoy painting and selling artwork outside of work.

- ⮑ Allows some people to pursue a hobby without having to rely on it for their primary income. A person who is part of a band may be a teacher during the week and play gigs on the weekend, for instance.

- ⮑ Some people fall into it (e.g., a teacher who is asked to do some tutoring).

- ⮑ To earn some additional income, such as a marketing assistant who earns a basic salary who could earn additional money by managing the social media of a small company in their spare time.

- ⮑ They need to have several sources of income for financial stability as one of their jobs does not pay them enough to cover all costs.

- ⮑ Often it can be to explore a business idea without the pressure of relying on it to work and support you full time.

It is not only people's desire to do what they love on the side that has led to a rise in the gig economy, but other factors have also played a part. Some of these are:

1. Companies are outsourcing more and more (outsourcing means finding people outside their company with specialized skills to complete a task/project for them rather than hiring them all year round).

2. Increasing numbers of business leaders claim to use a temporary workforce or interim professionals to support projects.

QUESTIONS

1. **What hobbies or interests do you have that may allow you to earn money in the future if you developed them?**

2. **Should you always turn hobbies into a source of income? Remember, some people do things for joy and trying to make money out of them is not joyful for them.**

Below I've listed some things to think about when answering the above questions:

- Knowing that you can pursue several things can be a relief for many young people, especially if they have a range of interests. Knowing that you don't have to pick a career at 16 and it will be the only thing you do for 40+ years is also a relief!

- As an example, a young person may want to be an electrician but also play in a band or teach music. You can be an electrician and a music tutor, working as an electrician during the day and tutoring outside of work hours, or even setting up a pre-recorded online course that earns you money while you work as an electrician.

- For other people, this may be a sign to think about what interests you and pursue other interests.

What are examples of a side hustle?

- **Drop Shipping -** This is where you provide (goods) by direct delivery from the manufacturer to the retailer or customer. So, you essentially promote goods and the company who makes them sends them to the customer while you make a percentage of the sales value.

- **Writing -** This might be writing the text for a website, brochure, or blogs, for instance. You need to have an area of interest/expertise in order to write well about it.

- **Desiging -** This might be t-shirts or graphic design material for websites or logo design, for instance. You can offer your services on websites like Fiverr and people will pay you for completed projects.

- **Blogging -** About an area of specialism, once this becomes popular you may charge for adverts (note your blog needs to be very popular first so it attracts a lot of traffic that advertisers then want to sell to), so you need to blog about an area of interest to you and preferably where you have reduced competition and can stand out.

- **Sell information products** (can be done with blogging) where you write eBooks in areas of specialism or produce online courses
- **Photography**
- **An additional part-time job to upskill**
- **Create your own products**

All the above will need you to be good at promoting what you're doing so you can find customers and opportunities.

So how do you develop a side hustle?

- Pick something you are passionate about because it's something you will have to spend your spare time on. You need to enjoy it.
- Identify your skills or the ones you want to build on.
- Think about your unfair advantages. Are you naturally good or interested in something, have you developed a skill that you can build on, do you have a family member who is particularly skilled in an area you'd like to learn about such as photography for instance and could you ask them to help you learn?
- Find people who are good at what you want to do and learn from them. This might involve doing courses, practicing, or studying their skills.
- Get feedback from other people who will be honest with you.
- Think about what you would like to buy/learn etc. and see if you can fulfill that need.
- Be prepared for it not to work overnight.

Below are some side hustles that turned into fully-fledged businesses. Research some of them and how they started. This will give you a feel for how some side hustles can become fully-fledged businesses. Research some of your own if these do not interest you.

- ⮑ **Cambridge Satchel Company** - Owner started the company in her kitchen with her mum in order to send her daughter to a better school.

- ⮑ **Under Armour** - Created t-shirts that were comfortable to wear during sport, while at college on the college football team.

- ⮑ **Yankee Candles** - The owner made his mum a candle with melted crayons at 16 and started getting orders from neighbours.

- ⮑ **The Khan Academy** - The owner made tutoring videos for his niece, and now they are one of the biggest online learning platforms.

- ⮑ **Twitter** - Developed as a result of a hackathon.

- ⮑ **Apple** - Started as a side hustle in a garage by its two co-founders whilst they had other jobs.

In Summary

A growing number of people rely on several sources of income to cover their wants and needs and also to pursue their interests. It is a good idea to explore how some of your interests could become a source of income either on the side along with your primary job or as a side hustle.

CHAPTER - 04

What Will Work Look Like in the Future?

In this chapter, we will look at:

- Predictions of how the workplace environment will look in the future
- The impact of artificial intelligence
- The move to skills over job title

One of the biggest challenges for parents, carers, and educators is trying to prepare young people for a world that doesn't exist yet. Adults in 2000 could not have foreseen how technology would change the workplace or predict the industries that have arisen because of it. (A careers advisor would not have told anyone to become an app developer for instance, as this was not a common job.) There is no crystal ball that allows us to say with 100% certainty what work will look like in the future. But some trends are taking place now that can give us some indications. You will find some listed below.

PWC in their report "Workforce of the Future"[11] suggests four possible scenarios to what the future of work will look like. Below I have tried to summarise these (please note this is my interpretation of them) and details of how to access the full report can be found in the footnotes.

Scenario 1: Red World

Sees a shift to small innovative businesses with few employees that are flexible and competitive. Work will be outsourced rather than hiring many people for a permanent job. Permanent employment will drop to an all-time low. Employees will pursue interests that will enable them to develop the latest ideas. Less of a distinction between young and old when it comes to business success, as the market will reward innovation and good ideas. Workers will not have the security of a stable job and will need a skill they are particularly strong in, as those who do will do very well for themselves.

Scenario 2: Blue World

Global corporations like Amazon, Microsoft etc. will become more powerful and gain the biggest profits because of their size. As a result, large mergers of companies will take place. Talented people at the top of their industry will be fought over and offered large salaries. Workers will be expected to work harder and perform better, and in exchange, companies will provide additional childcare and health services so workers can focus on work.

Scenario 3: Green World

Businesses with a social purpose will have the biggest advantage. They will care about the planet, human rights, diversity etc. Success for a business will depend on the company culture so it can attract the right people to work for it and customers who like the brand. Employees will be held to high ethical standards and their social media will play a big part in that.

Scenario 4: Yellow World

Workers will give the company meaning and drive it forward. There will be a lot of autonomy, allowing workers to work on projects they are passionate about. Workers will form bodies like trade unions that are guided by what they can contribute to society and also look after members.

---

11   Price Waterhouse Cooopers, Workforce of the Future – The competing forces shaping 2030, https://www.pwc.com/gx/en/services/people-organisation/publications/workforce-of-the-future.html

THE WORLD OF WORK

QUESTIONS

1. Which world would you want to work in? Why?
2. Is there a world that you would not want to work in at all? Why?
3. Which one do you think is most likely?

As you can see, the worlds above are quite different, and as highlighted at the beginning of this chapter, it is incredibly difficult to imagine exactly how the world of work will change in 10 years, although we know it is changing.

Artificial intelligence (AI):

Artificial Intelligence is the development of computer systems able to perform tasks normally requiring human intelligence, such as visual perception, speech recognition, decision-making, and translation between languages.

AI has the power to make numerous jobs obsolete (no longer needed), in particular those that have repetitive tasks. These jobs can often be completed by machinery as they are repetitive, and a machine can be programmed to do them repeatedly. Ever been on a website and a chat box pops up from a customer services representative offering to help? Chances are it's not a human, but a script that looks for keywords in your question and then gives you a predetermined answer. The website owners know what the most popular questions are by customers and can programme these in with standard responses. Thus, they do not need to recruit hundreds of customer service people. Other jobs at risk of disappearing include drivers and if driverless cars/trucks are in place. Restaurants in Japan have already tried waiters that are robots.

However, artificial intelligence is also argued to create many jobs in the future. The world will need:

- ➲ Engineers
- ➲ Lawyers specialising in ethics, as new technology can often pose ethical challenges. Just because we can do something doesn't mean we should.
- ➲ Graphic designers
- ➲ Marketers and public relations experts selling new products as a result of AI and also to communicate the ethics of AI advances to customers.

➲ Computer programmers

➲ Data analysts

The changing workplace

COVID-19 has already shown us that people can work from home and the number of companies likely to move towards flexible working (allowing employees to work from home or come into the office when needed). As more and more cities make travelling to work in a car difficult, in order to reduce pollution and climate change (London has introduced new charges to drive in the city and outer London, Oxford is largely pedestrianised as is central Nottingham), this will encourage more companies to take this action.

Flexibility

Workplaces will offer the flexibility of hours but will also expect flexibility from workers, which may include working long hours and weekends to get projects completed, followed by breaks. The 9 am-5 pm, 5 days a week structure may well become a thing of the past.

Position won't matter as much as skill.

We have seen a move away from hierarchical organisational structures (where job titles determine how much power and authority you have, as well as your pay). Google, for example, questioned whether it needed managers at all and resisted them for several years, arguing that they hire very intelligent people who don't need managing. As the projects they take on become more diverse and complex, they have introduced a management structure but to a limited extent, and it remains very flat in its structure. It is predicted that this move will continue, and workers will be rewarded based on their expertise and results rather than job title and length of service. And therefore will have an increasing personal stake in the success of their work because they will gain bigger rewards the more successful it is.

In Summary

It is impossible to know exactly how the world of work will look in 10 years. However, we can make some predictions based on the changes we are already seeing. We know things that are likely to change, including the workplace, the size and shape of companies, and the contract under which people are recruited. It is important to keep an eye on these so that young people can adapt to these changes.

CHAPTER - 05

Learning in the Future

In this chapter, we will look at:

- How learning during a person's lifetime is changing
- Different methods/times of learning and re-skilling and their advantages and disadvantages
- The soft skills that employers are looking for

The traditional path of learning is changing. Learning 20 years ago looked like this. A child may or may not go to nursery before progressing to primary school and then secondary. After their GCSEs, they would decide to do A levels or other technical qualifications or go into work. They then may decide to go to university if they have the necessary qualifications.

Changes in the way people are learning, upskilling, and what future learning may look like

The earlier parts of a young person's education are likely to look much the same with nursery, primary, and secondary education to give them foundational knowledge in the basic disciplines such as maths, science, English, languages, the humanities, and the arts. At this point, young people may choose between A Levels, Btecs, the new government introduced T Levels, or go into work. If they decide to complete further education after their GCSEs, they may or may not go to complete Level 4 or 5 qualifications, complete an apprenticeship, or find work. However, a key change taking place is when people decide to do degrees and the number of people taking higher-level qualifications later in their career. In 2019/20, there were around 254,000 mature undergraduate entrants at UK universities; 37% of all undergraduate entrants.[12]

We have discussed in the previous chapter how young people can expect to have several jobs and careers and, in many cases, this will require retraining. It will become commonplace for Lawyers to retrain as accountants taking exams after 20 years in the workplace if they so wish. Engineers may switch to architecture. The use of skills will become more fluid.

In May 2021, the UK Government pledged to introduce a Skills and Post 16 Education Bill to support a lifetime skills guarantee. This would mean that every adult could access a flexible loan for higher-level education usable at any point in their lives. It also puts employers under pressure to provide publicly funded training programmes through a skills accelerator programme. This is at the same time as we have seen the introduction of the new T Level courses, which are pitched as more job-relevant.

The above gives a clear indication of the changing face of education and that upskilling and learning will become a lifelong matter rather than something one does only in their teens.

---

12   House of Commons Library, Mature students in England, https://commonslibrary.parliament.uk/research-briefings/cbp-8809/

THE WORLD OF WORK

List as many reasons as possible as to why this shift in learning is necessary. Why might a person want to get additional qualifications/continue with their learning?

1.
2.
3.
4.

Some reasons for gaining qualifications throughout your working career are:

- ➲ Changing technology means we need to constantly upskill.
- ➲ Some people learn better as they get older, so they may prefer to study further as they get older.
- ➲ New industries are starting up which need specialist skills.
- ➲ Some people are not sure what they want to do when they are younger. As this becomes clearer throughout their career, lifelong learning allows them to get the relevant qualifications for their chosen career later in life.
- ➲ It is impossible to learn everything you need in a two-year A level course or three-year degree, for instance, therefore developing your learning is necessary.
- ➲ By providing training, the company shows you how much they appreciate you and your skills.

List three benefits of taking qualifications throughout your career.

1.	
2.	
3.	

Again, some are listed below:

- Companies will often pay for these courses to upskill you. This can be cheaper than when you are doing them yourself.
- After being in a career, you may want to specialise in a certain area. There is no way to know this until you start your career, so a degree later in life or a top-up qualification is the perfect way to upskill.
- An investment in a person's training often shows that the company is committed to keeping them.
- Allows you to be more effective at work, thus giving you greater satisfaction.
- Often recognised courses that are externally examined are a building block for promotions.
- The completion of a course may come with a financial reward and increased salary.

QUESTION

Are there any drawbacks to learning throughout your career?

The main one is the time pressure it puts on the employees who are trying to work and learn at the same time (employees should be given some time to complete the qualification if their company has put them on the course, but this can be difficult in practical terms.) Some people who have been out of learning for several years forget how to revise or learn, and it can be a challenge to get back into it.

If a person doesn't always need to have all their qualifications before they apply for a job, then what are employers looking for?

A basic level of qualification will always be necessary to do well in the workplace. So ensuring you have a good grasp of language, mathematical skills, scientific principles, and humanities, as well as being creative, will give you a solid foundation to build a career upon. However, specialisation, such as that seen at degree level, is starting to take place in the workplace.

Employers also value soft skills. Below are some of the soft skills that they look out for.

- Communication skills
- Enthusiasm and a positive attitude
- Teamwork
- Networking and the ability to speak to people that you may not know well or normally interact with
- Critical thinking/problem solving
- Professionalism in demeanour and physical and written communication

a. Identify where opportunities to develop the above soft skills present themselves in your life. This may be in or out of school. For instance, classroom presentations give you public speaking skills. You may be part of a sports team to build up team working skills, etc.

b. Rate yourself from 1 (low) to 10 (very well developed) for each of the skills. Most people excel in some over others. What should you be working on?

In Summary

People will most likely continue to gain qualifications throughout their careers in order to upskill themselves. This is already happening. However, with the rise in technology, this transition is likely to become more dominant, as it allows people to gain qualifications outside of work hours and without having to travel. Employers are also looking for softer skills, and these are something young people need to be focused on developing as well.

Conclusion

The world is changing—it always has. But young people need to know that these changes are happening at a faster pace than ever before. The certainties that the previous generations relied on are long gone. Ideas around retirement, recruitment, spending and saving habits are all changing. The gap between the rich and the poor is widening, and we can no longer leave financial literacy up to chance or the hope that young people will figure it out as they go along.

This book was written for two audiences but with one purpose.

The audiences are:

- Young people themselves: to give them access to a digestible amount of financial knowledge in a simple way and with lots of food for thought.
- Parents, Carers and Teachers: no matter what their own level of financial literacy, who can work through the book with their young people.

The purpose:

Unlike a traditional textbook, I hope you dip in and out of this several times. Applying for a credit card? I hope you read the section on credit and debit cards before you pick one. Picking a savings account? I hope you flick to that page in the book too. The information provided isn't everything there is to know about money, the workplace, or the economy. However, it's here to level the playing field just a little, to ensure that we all have the basic principles covered.

I wish you the best.

Printed in Great Britain
by Amazon

78493115R00099